Travels

of

Samuel McIlvaine

1862

EX LIBRIS

COLLEGII DAVIDSONIENSIS

Presented in memory of

Joseph Abrams Bailey
Class of 1878

by

Mrs. Helen Bailey Obering

An Endowed Fund

BY THE DIM AND FLARING LAMPS:

I have seen Him in the watchfires
of a hundred circling camps;
They have builded Him an altar
in the evening dews and damps;
I can read His righteous sentence
by the dim and flaring lamps.
　　His day is marching on.
　　Glory! glory hallelujah!
　　Glory! Glory hallelujah!
　　Glory! Glory hallelujah!
　　His truth is marching on.

The Battle Hymn of the Republic
Julia Ward Howe

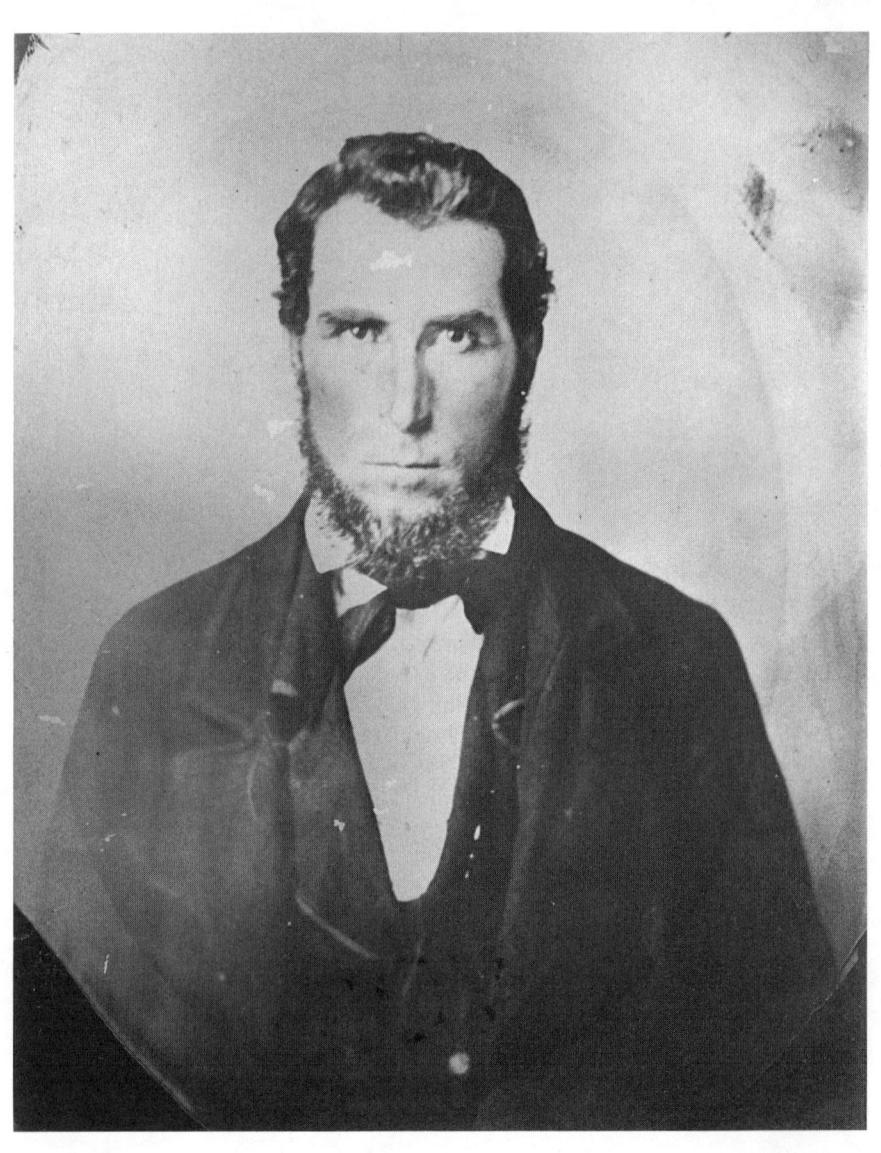

Samuel McIlvaine

By

The dim

And Flaring Lamps:

The Civil War diaries of

Samuel McIlvaine

edited by
Clayton E. Cramer

Library Research Associates Inc.
Monroe, New York
1990

973.78
M152b

© Copyright 1990
Clayton E. Cramer

Printed in the United States of America. All rights reserved. Permission to reprint or to reproduce in any form must be obtained in writing from the publisher, except for review excerpts.

Library Research Associates, Inc.
Dunderberg Road RD#5, Box 41
Monroe, New York 10950

Library of Congress Cataloging-in-Publication Data:

McIlvaine, Samuel, b 1824-d.1863
 By the dim and flaring lamps : the Civil War diaries of Samuel McIlvaine / edited by Clayton E. Cramer.
 167p. cm.
ISBN: 0-912526-46-7 : $28.95

1. McIlvaine, Samuel, 1824-1863—Diaries. 2. United States—History—Civil War, 1861-1865—Diaries. 3. Soldiers—Indiana—Benton County—Diaries. 4. Benton County (Ind.)—Biography. I. Cramer, Clayton E. II. Title.
E601.M35 1990
973.7'81—dc20

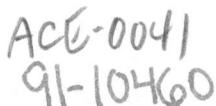

To
the memory of
my father,
Edwin Frederick Cramer

TABLE OF CONTENTS

Introduction	1
Letter of January 21, 1862	9
The Diary	17
February Entries	18
March Entries	48
April Entries	86
May Entries	104
June Entries	136
Letter of September 29, 1862	140
Bibliography	149
Index	151

Illustrations credit:

Harper's Pictorial History of the Great Rebellion of the U.S., 1866, Harper & Brothers

Sgt. Samuel McIlvaine

Introduction

It appears that Samuel sent his diary to his family periodically, perhaps as he filled each volume. The material in this book (with the exception of the two letters home) covers a little over five months; Samuel's entry of February 27, 1862, indicates that he was sending home a diary covering his previous time in the Army. Unfortunately, only this one volume was passed down through my branch of the family. Does another volume of his diary sit in an attic somewhere, slowly rotting away? It frustrates me to think so, and not be able to find it.

It appears that Samuel's son Silas McIlvaine inherited the diary. In turn, Silas passed the diary to his daughter, Hazel McIlvaine Meacham. Hazel's sister Jessie McIlvaine Cramer, my paternal grandmother, transcribed the manuscript in the late 1950s, faithfully reproducing every spelling error, punctuation mark, and nonstandard use of English.

When Jessie McIlvaine Cramer died in 1971, my interest in genealogy and history made me the logical recipient of the diary, even though I was only 15. The diary sat on my bookshelf as a family heirloom for several years, occasionally read, but more commonly a conversation piece.

INTRODUCTION

My love for history is largely the result of my father's efforts; when he died in 1976, I could think of no more fitting tribute to him than to edit Samuel's diary into a readable form.

Other than what we learn of Samuel in the pages of this diary, we know almost nothing of his life. This is especially embarrassing since he married into a family for which we have a tremendous wealth of information.

Samuel married Margaret Jane McConnell sometime between 1845 and 1850 in Benton County, Indiana; they lived on a farm in that area until Samuel enlisted in the 10th Indiana Volunteer Infantry Regiment. Samuel and Margaret had a total of four children: Silas, Anah, Sara, and William, all of whom survived infancy. After Samuel left for the war, Margaret moved to Oxford, county seat of Benton.[1]

His descriptions throughout the diary of soil, crops, and farm tools suggest that he was a farmer. The letter of September 29th to his mother indicates that he was a devout Christian, and felt a moral imperative to participate in the war.

---

[1] Ethel McConnell Bartindale, *McConnell Family History*, (Oxford, Indiana: privately printed, 1923), pp. 24-25.

BY THE DIM AND FLARING LAMPS:
THE CIVIL WAR DIARY OF SAMUEL MCILVAINE

Samuel's description of the Ohio River:

It would seem hardly necessary to speak of the towns and scenery along this well known river; yet as these jottings may fall into the hands of some who like myself have but a poor idea of the views along this river, I will devote a few lines to a brief description.

suggests that he realized the potential historical significance of the diary, as well as his detailed descriptions of common objects, such as a cotton gin. There are other clues that suggest Samuel realized the significance of his diary: his care in making distinctions between rumor and what he knew to be true; his desire to understate the details of the incident of March 26, 1862 to compensate for probable exaggeration; his explanation of facts widely known at the time that he wrote (*e.g.*, referring to John Bell as "... one of the recent candidates for President of the United States").

I was somewhat surprised by Samuel's entry of February 8th, in which he correctly identifies the process by which stalactites and stalagmites form. I would be surprised if most college graduates today would be able to explain it -- and Samuel was a farmer, already an adult, in an era when mandatory primary schooling was just becoming common in the United States.

Samuel's feelings about slavery aren't stated explicitly -- in fact, his diary seems unnaturally obtuse on the subject. His February 18th account of the slave hunters, and his March 4th entry describing his conversation with a slave:

INTRODUCTION

This Negro seemed to think the war was somehow to result in favor of the slaves, or some way to their advantage, despite the tales their masters told them of the horrible treatment they were to receive from the Yankees. He also said he thought he ought to be free, and felt fully able to provide for and take care of himself.

seem to go out of their way to avoid expressing an opinion on slavery. Since Samuel's diary was intended to be read by his family, he may have been avoiding controversial opinions -- especially since there seems to be some evidence in his letter of September 29th that his mother disapproved of his participation in the war.

This disapproval may have been out of concern for Samuel's family, the very natural desire of a mother to not see her son die on a battlefield, or political in nature. The simplistic accounts of the Civil War most of us learned in primary and secondary schools tend to overlook the significant disagreements in the North concerning the War, slavery, and the relative position of blacks and whites in society. It would not be surprising if Samuel avoided writing opinions that would be controversial back home in Indiana, a state whose Constitution prohibited both slavery and free blacks from entering the state[2], and a state with "... more people of Southern ancestry or Southern sympathies ... than in any other free state."[3]

Samuel was astonishingly good humored about the miserable conditions of field life. Consider his March 31st entry:

---

[2] Bruce Catton, *Glory Road*, (Garden City: Doubleday & Co., 1952), p. 113.
[3] Catton, p. 115.

BY THE DIM AND FLARING LAMPS:
THE CIVIL WAR DIARY OF SAMUEL MCILVAINE

> Among other things on the table was lettuce, the first green thing I have tasted this spring (if I except spoiled meat).

Throughout the diary, Samuel expresses a child-like faith in his government, its leaders, and the military justice system. In his March 10th entry Samuel writes:

> I learn, however, that Col. Manson's trial comes on today, and further that he has instituted a suit of enquiry, or an investigation of the allegations against him, when if they [are] found to be unjust or untrue the case will, of course, be dismissed.

We know just a little more about Samuel's death. He is reported to have died September 8, 1863, and probably died near Stevenson, Alabama, where he was initially buried. At the time of death, he was a sergeant. His remains were later moved to the Chattanooga National Cemetery in Tennessee.[4] Family tradition holds that he died after a "30-foot fall while exploring a saltpeter cave with some comrades".[5] Several entries in his diary describe cave explorations in which he participated; it would not be surprising if he actually met his end in this manner.

As the title suggests, Samuel McIlvaine made the entries in his journal with poor lighting, during rainstorms, and while seriously ill. None of these circumstances are well-suited to consistent spelling, handwriting, punctuation, or paragraphing; nonetheless, the resulting manuscript required less editing than I originally expected.

---

[4] Curtis W. Spence, Superintendent, Chattanooga National Cemetery, Letter to Jessie McIlvaine Cramer, 28 December 1960.
[5] Bartindale, p. 24.

INTRODUCTION

Punctuation throughout the diary is haphazard; sentences as long as eighty words were common in the original. While I have altered the author's punctuation as little as possible to avoid distorting Samuel's meaning, it was necessary to simplify some non-stop sentences to a more comprehensible form. Where there was uncertainty in my mind as to the intent of the author's punctuation, it has not been altered.

For the most part, Samuel McIlvaine's spelling was both consistent and modern. Many words were spelled consistently in the British manner (*e.g.*, neighbour, colour), which was not uncommon into the early parts of this century. In the interests of readability, I have used modern American spelling.

The spelling of names was more troublesome. The *correct* spelling of place names do change, and the *correct* spelling of a person's name is frequently at variance with how that individual spells his name. For these reasons, where Samuel's spelling of a place name does not match the current spelling, I have included the current spelling in the notes. In addition, because many of these villages are too small to show up on large scale maps (and some readers may want to follow along on a map), I have included the county and state in brackets for place names where Samuel did not include this information. Unless I was able to find evidence that Samuel's spelling of a person's name was wrong, I have left the spelling "as is". Where there is uncertainty as to which of several officers by a particular name and rank are meant, I have listed the first names of all officers that seem likely. Unless otherwise noted, all

BY THE DIM AND FLARING LAMPS:
THE CIVIL WAR DIARY OF SAMUEL MCILVAINE

military units identified by state name and number are regiments.

Throughout the diary, certain collective nouns that we think of as singular, such as *regiment*, are used by the author in the plural. While at first this sounds unusual ("Most of our regiment were yet in bed"), it also reminds us that Samuel viewed the regiment as a group of individuals, not an entity of its own. Consequently, I have left these occurrences in their original number.

Not surprisingly, many sentences start in one tense and end in another. In the interest of readability, the tenses have been made consistent.

Very few words have completely fallen out of use; where they have, it is frequently because the action performed or the object described is no longer a part of our world. More commonly, the primary meaning in Samuel's day has become a secondary meaning today (e.g., *teamster*; referring to a driver of horses). In a few cases, Samuel used nonstandard English which remains to this day understandable (e.g., *suspicioned* for *suspected*).

Throughout the diary, Samuel underlined words. In some cases for emphasis: "*Steam* (what will it not be made to do yet)...". In other cases to express sarcasm: "...the Capitol house for the 'lower class' *assembly* of the State of Indiana (penitentiary)". I have taken the liberty of italicizing where Samuel underlined, since it seems clear that Samuel would have done the same in type.

My objective in annotating this diary is to enhance the reader's understanding of the events, people, and places referred to in the diary. A historian of the Civil War is likely

INTRODUCTION

to find my notes superfluous and shallow; nonspecialists will not. It was necessary to decide which events, people, and places were sufficiently well-known that no notes were required. In general, I have made this decision by the simple rule that, if I was familiar with it, it must be well-known.

A great many people deserve recognition for their assistance in editing Samuel McIlvaine's diary and researching the notes. I want to take this occasion to thank my late grandmother, Jessie McIlvaine Cramer, whose painstaking transcription of the manuscript in the late 1950s made it possible for me to concentrate on editing the text and researching the notes; my wife, Rhonda, for encouraging me to continue when more financially rewarding opportunities distracted me from this book; Professor Daniel Markwyn of Sonoma State University, whose encouragement and enthusiasm started me on this project; Professor Million of Purdue University, for assisting me in locating one maddeningly obscure fact about Senator Graham Fitch; and my colleagues Charlyn Johnson and Susan Lapping for reviewing my manuscript and making suggestions at a time when too many years of reading the same words had blinded me to awkward sentences and gross misspellings.

Letter Of January 21, 1862

In the following letter (written sixteen days before the first diary entry), Samuel describes his part in the Battle of Logan's Cross Roads, also know as the Battle of Fishing Creek, fought on January 19, 1862. This letter was written on the back, front, and margins of a captured Confederate document.

**Gen. Zollicoffer's Camp
on the Cumberland River
near Sommerset, Pulaski County, Kentucky
January 21, 1862**

J. B. Willson

Dear Nephew:
I gladly received your letter of the 3rd January on the 17th ... which informs me your family are just getting over the measles. I trust this will find you and your family well. I am quite well, and have been with slight exceptions since I entered the army.
When we made our hasty advent into Kentucky the right wing of our regiment went immediately down the Louisville and Nashville Railroad to the Rolling Fork Salt River, to where the rebels had burned the bridge a few days before. [We] guarded the [rail]road and men for about a week while repairing the bridge, thence to Bardstown [seat of

LETTER OF JANUARY 21, 1862

Nelson County, Kentucky], where joining the other wing of our regiment, we overawed the Disunion element, & kept the peace for over a month, during which time we were busily drilling. We then made our first march south striking the Lebanon Branch Road at New Haven [Nelson County, Kentucky], hardly got camped here until we were ordered to Lebanon, Marion County [Kentucky]. Here we remained until the last December drilling and awaiting the organizing of the Union forces. Whilst here we received the news daily, and quickly got our letters from our friends, but were finally ordered to Columbus, Adair County [probably Columbia, Adair County, Kentucky].

When we start[ed] for that place, we took leave of railroads and telegraph, of daily news, and decreased the facilities for receiving letters from our friends. It was here, Lebanon, we had our coldest weather, freezing the ground two inches deep; here too we had our only snow worth noticing, which melted off in two days. We had a pretty good pike to Columbus and got along finely. Here we stayed but a day or two, and started eastward to Sommerset, Pulaski County, [Kentucky]. On this march we began fully to appreciate the difficulties of marching an army over about the worst and muddiest roads I ever passed over for so long a distance. The distance between Columbia & Sommerset is about 35 miles over a low level swampy clayey soil, covered most[ly] with a kind of scrubby blackjack timber or brush, the balance of the way very broken and hilly. I would [not] give my place, or yours, for 20 miles square of such country. I asked some of the people through here, the price of the land. They said when times were better before the war it sold at one dollar per acre.

Imagine a considerable army [of] several thousand troops, with a train of wagons of a hundred or two hundred drawn by four horses or six mules floundering & plunging through the mud, the wagons often up to the axles, the teams frequently down or stuck fast, prying up wagons, cutting roads around etc. and you will have a slight idea of our march.

BY THE DIM AND FLARING LAMPS:
THE CIVIL WAR DIARY OF SAMUEL MCILVAINE

Samuel's account is not the traditional grousing of the foot soldier; official accounts of this march record that one 40-mile march required eight days because of the mud.[1]

After near a week we camped in a field or open ground about nine or ten miles from Sommerset on the east and about seven or eight miles from [the] Zollicoffer encampment on the Cumberland River. Here we expected to form a junction with the forces under Gen. Schoepf (which have been at Sommerset for some time) and prepare for attacking Zollicoffer, who has also been here for about six weeks, collecting his forces, entrenching, & fortifying. Up to this time we had hardly seen an enemy, who was openly so; but during our first night here, we had an alarm about midnight, but it turned out to be nothing more than the firing of the pickets of each army upon each other, and the regiment which had been called out of our bunks, and formed in line of battle were dismissed to their beds again.

Union Brig. Gen. Albin Francisco Schoepf (1822-1886): Born in Hungary, Schoepf was an officer with the Prussian Army until he was exiled to Turkey in 1848. After serving with the Ottoman Army, Schoepf immigrated to the United States, where he worked for the Coast Survey and the Patent Office before the war.[2]

Confederate Brig. Gen. Felix Kirk Zollicoffer (1812-1862): Before the war Zollicoffer had been both a newspaper publisher and editor in Tennessee and Kentucky. From 1844-1849 Zollicoffer was Tennessee State

---

[1] Mark M. Boatner III, *The Civil War Dictionary* (New York: David McKay Company, Inc., 1959), p. 488.
[2] Boatner, p. 726.

LETTER OF JANUARY 21, 1862

Controller; from 1853-1859 he sat in the House of Representatives for Tennessee.[3]

We had hardly expected that Old "Zollie" as the boys have been in the habit of calling him, would venture out of his position to attack us, but it seems that either through spies or other means, they got the idea that there was but a regiment or two of us with a considerable train of wagons, and they would come up and cut us off and capture the wagons, and so on Sunday morn last the 19th ... at daylight they were upon us some seven or eight thousand strong from the best information we could get. Most of our regiment were yet in bed when the long roll [call to battle] was beat. [Soon] we were up, dressed, seized our guns & cartridge boxes, and were formed in line of battle and marched some 1/2 mile from camp into a dense woods where we met them with a volley from our whole line. They were in an open field at the edge of the woods and returned the fire immediately. Our regiment sustained their fire alone for almost an hour when the 4th Kentucky formed on our left, but before this a retreat was ordered, but from some misunderstanding of the command, or other reason, only the right wing at first fell back and that only partially and in Indian style, loading and firing from behind trees as we went.

The woods were so dense that we could only occasionally see an enemy. When our men began to fall back, for which [they] could not see any good reason, I began to think the tale was about told. I felt much vexed and chagrined, to think our men were running, for as I was some distance in advance of most of them I did not hear the order to retreat, and you may be sure this feeling was not lessened when the rebels thinking they had routed us raised a yell of delight. The ordering of a retreat was perhaps, as I afterwards learned, well, as they were flanking us on the right. But they soon had reason to know that they were sadly mistaken, the falling back of our men on the right drew them to the left where the Kentucky 4th was forming, and the Ohio 9th, and Minnesota 2nd coming to our relief about the same time.

---

3 "Zollicoffer, Felix Kirk", *Encyclopedia Americana*, 1963, XXIX, p. 722.

BY THE DIM AND FLARING LAMPS:
THE CIVIL WAR DIARY OF SAMUEL MCILVAINE

They were soon taught that they were under a very great error, when they thought they had whipped us.

Col. [Speed S.] Fry of the 4th Kentucky met [Zollicoffer] face to face, knew him and shot him through the breast. Several of their colonels and captains were killed or taken prisoners, and it is thought, but of this I am not certain, that Gen. Crittenden is our prisoner. They were completely routed leaving their generals dead on the field, as well as many others of their officers and many more [who] were officers were taken. Their loss in killed and wounded must have been from 400 to 500, probably more. As we pursued them immediately I had no chance to learn much about it. I think, though, on the part of the field I was on I must have seen in killed, wounded, and prisoners, as many as 50.

Col. (later Brig. Gen.) Speed S. Fry (1817-92): Fry served in the Mexican War; worked as lawyer and judge afterwards, and organized the 4th Kentucky Infantry in late 1861.[4]

Samuel's account of this incident is nowhere near as peculiar as history records it to be. Gen. Zollicoffer met Fry while Fry was reconnoitering near the front. Because Zollicoffer's white raincoat hid his uniform, Fry at first believed the stranger who claimed Fry's men were firing at each other. Another Confederate rode up and shot Fry's horse, at which point Fry and several Union soldiers shot Zollicoffer. By one account Gen. Zollicoffer was attempting get the upper hand by persuading Fry to cease fire;[5] other accounts indicate that Zollicoffer was nearsighted and honestly thought that Fry's men were Confederate soldiers.

---

[4] Boatner, p. 319.
[5] Boatner, p. 488.

LETTER OF JANUARY 21, 1862

The Confederate attack was not well coordinated, and Gen. Thomas' troops had been reinforced just before the battle by three regiments and a battery from Gen. Schoepf without the Confederates being aware of it. Zollicoffer's Tennessee regiments were also disadvantaged by flintlock muskets that would not fire in the rain.[6]

The Battle of Fishing Creek was a serious reversal for the Confederacy. Many of Crittenden's troops deserted because of the battle, including two entire regiments.[7]

Confederate Gen. George B. Crittenden (1812-1880) commanded Zollicoffer's and W. H. Carroll's brigades at the Battle of Mill Spring. He was *not* taken prisoner in this battle.[8] Gen. Crittenden was a senior officer of the Regular Army who resigned in 1861 to join the Confederacy.

Gen. Crittenden was from one of those Kentucky families split apart by the war. His father, John J. Crittenden, had worked to keep Kentucky in the Union. George's younger brother, Brig. Gen. Thomas L. Crittenden, commanded a division in the Union Army under Gen. Don Carlos Buell.[9] Gen. Crittenden had a drinking problem, twice resigning from the U. S. Army to avoid court-martial for drunkeness on duty, and being dismissed after that for the same reason. Gen. Bragg (Crittenden's superior) ordered Crittenden removed from his command for drunkeness and incompetence on March 31st.[10]

---

[6] Wiley Sword, *Shiloh: Bloody April*, (New York: William Morrow & Company, 1974), p. 60-61.
[7] Sword, p. 508-509.
[8] Boatner, p. 208.
[9] Sword, p. 60.
[10] Sword, p. 86.

BY THE DIM AND FLARING LAMPS:
THE CIVIL WAR DIARY OF SAMUEL MCILVAINE

I had the pleasure or honor, (or whatever you choose to call it) [of] leading three of them up to where they could be guarded, two Mississippians, and one from Tennessee. From one of them I took a loaded Colt's revolver.

I learn from some of our men who came in from the battlefield this eve, eleven men of our regiment were killed and 50 wounded; of our company but one man was wounded & he slightly; the whole loss on our side was 35 killed and 127 wounded.

Union losses in this battle were actually 39 killed, 207 wounded.[11]

As we followed them up to their camp, we had hardly started when it became evident they had made a perfect stampede, wagon loads of blankets, haversacks filled with provisions, were left strewn along the road for miles. As we had started without breakfast, we made a hearty meal from theirs.

We approached their camp near sundown; our [artillerymen] fired their guns and threw a few shells into their camp. They replied by two or three shot; as dark came on we ceased firing [and] lay on our arms until morning.

Infantrymen rested on their rifles or muskets if the ground was wet and there was no opportunity to pitch tents.[12]

It was suspicioned during the night that they were retreating across the river; as soon as it became light this was confirmed. We could see them crossing with a small steamboat, some swimming their

---

[11] Boatner, p. 489.
[12] John D. Billings, *Hardtack and Coffee or The Unwritten Story of Army Life*, (Williamstown, MA: Corner House Publishers, 1973), p. 348.

LETTER OF JANUARY 21, 1862

horses. The guns were fixed on the boat and soon it was in flames. We started for their camp about a mile [away], found but one living man in it. All of their cannon, fourteen in number, about 300 wagons and over 1000 horses & mules fell into our hands. In their shanties (evidently prepared for wintering) we are now snugly ensconced [settled], where we found everything ready to our hands for living.
Yours Truly,
S. McIlvaine

Samuel was correct about the number of horses and mules, and close about the number of artillery pieces; 12 guns and caissons were captured, along with 150 wagons.[13]

It is hardly necessary for me to say that this letter is written on a rebel document and with rebel ink found in their camp. Even the envelope is rebel. We left everything of this kind at our camp. They have, however, come in this evening. I would write further of the particulars but our [postmaster] goes out in a few minutes with our letters. I hope soon to hear from you again. I have not seen Dr. Thompson since leaving Lebanon as he was in the Hospital Dept. but learn he was about to get a discharge from the service. Write direct to Company D, 10th Indiana Regiment, Kentucky.

S. Mc.

---

[13] Boatner, p. 489.

The Diary

To my Family

and

Friends

I send this further continuation

of my Diary, or daily journal

being

a plain and unvarnished statement of facts, which

came under my daily observation; and with which I

was

connected, in the Army

With occasional reflections and observations.

Sam'l McIlvaine

February Entries

Wednesday, February 5, 1862
Mill Springs, Kentucky

Weather very fine, sun shines all day. I spend a part of the day in writing etc. but the most important feature of the day was an imposing drill we had this afternoon, the first we have had for some time, and I think undertaken as much to show our skill and prowess as to give us a little exercise and an airing. [We] drilled in a large field to south of camp, went through the skirmish drill, with many other maneuvers and evolutions in good order bringing us to our wind nicely; wound up by forming line of battle and discharging our pieces. The balls striking a parallel string of fence near a half mile distant, were plainly distinguished, and told but too plainly the danger to an enemy which should occupy a position where the fence stood. After the drill [we] had our first dress parade since the battle.

Thursday, February 6, 1862

Rained heavily in the night, with severe thunder and lightning. Sun came out this morn but is soon hid again.

Near midnight last night we were suddenly aroused by the beating of the long roll [call to battle]. It was pouring down rain and so dark that we could hardly distinguish each other. Nevertheless we sprung up instantly, jerking on such articles of clothing as had been taken off on lying down, some not even getting these in the dark & hurry & confusion, [as] the urgency seemed to increase. Sergeants and other officers calling to the men to "fall out", "get into line" etc. in tones and expressions, (not to say expletives) that seemed to indicate that the enemy were on the point of entering the camp, commencing an indiscriminate slaughter. I got my clothing on, snatched my cartridge box & gun, rushed out.

BY THE DIM AND FLARING LAMPS:
THE CIVIL WAR DIARY OF SAMUEL MCILVAINE

We were marched by companies speedily to the rebel entrenchments, or earthen breastworks, determined to turn their labor to the best advantage for our protection, and give them cause to regret ever having erected them; here we stood in the pouring rain and soft clay and mud, steadily and silently listening for the approach of the enemy for at least an hour. Some of the men in the hurry ran out without their caps, others without shoes or boots, and many without oilcloth or overcoat, among these latter was I. A moment would have sufficed to get my oilcloth, but the confusion was so great, and the urgency seeming to increase, I went without, and of course got thoroughly soaked from hand to foot. Many who were really sick, and had been in bed most of the time of late, also jumped up, seized their [gear] and rushed out. It was finally ascertained, or concluded, that the alarm was false and we were dismissed to our quarters having caught nothing worse than a heavy shower of rain, instead of a shower of lead.

It is said this morning, that the alarm was caused by the firing of some of Wolford's Calvary [First Kentucky Calvary[1]] who were returning from a scout, and supposed themselves out of hearing of camp. Our situation was indeed an unenviable one, had the enemy been cognizant of it, (and who could say they were not, as citizens who might be spies were passing through and about our camp every day) and collected their scattered forces, and made a bold dash upon us in the night. The river was very high, and crossing even in the daylight a tedious and difficult matter with the means we had at command. Our regiment were all the troops we had on the south side of the river (except two companies of the 10th Kentucky who crossed yesterday evening) without a single piece of artillery on this side. Notwithstanding (as I learn) Hosskin's Regiment [Kentucky 12th] with perhaps some other troops are on this side [of] the river, but opposite Sommerset, too far off to render immediate assistance, therefore we were in a good situation to be cut to pieces or captured had the enemy rallied his forces and fell upon us suddenly; but it appears this was

---

1 Boatner, p. 488.

very far from their thoughts, having already received one severe lesson, in undertaking to surprise us.

Nothing of consequence occurred in camp today, except that the 10th Kentucky [Infantry] Regiment or the balance of them cross over the river and prepare to take up their quarters in the new camp the rebels were fitting up to the east of us across the ravine.

Col. Harlan of the Kentucky 10th [Infantry] appears to be a determined, energetic and working man. Whilst moving his regiment over today, he not only managed and superintended the business, but laid hold and helped draw the boat across, which was done by means of a cable stretched across the river; while standing on the bank observing their operations, the rope which the Col. had hold of being forced down stream by the current suddenly rebounded, jerking the Col. over the bow of the boat into the river. He was, however, caught by the legs as he went over by one or two of the men, and drawn back, minus his cap.

John Marshall Harlan (1833-1911): A lawyer before the war, he later served as Attorney General of Kentucky from 1863 to 1866. He was appointed Associate Justice of the U.S. Supreme Court in 1877, and served on the Bering Sea Tribunal of Arbitration in 1893. Samuel's perception of Col. Harlan was obviously shared by others.[2]

February 7, 1862

Gloomy and rainy again today.

Come[s] my turn to go on guard today. Whilst not standing on duty spend the time in writing etc.

Mud seems to be the prevailing element in this most disgusting and filthy place. Many are already sick and other are taking sick every

---

[2] "Harlan, John Marshall", *Encyclopedia Americana*, 1963, XIII, pp. 709-710.

BY THE DIM AND FLARING LAMPS:
THE CIVIL WAR DIARY OF SAMUEL MCILVAINE

day. Some of those who are sick get rapidly worse; the principal surgeon is at Campbellsville [seat of Taylor County, Kentucky], under arrest and most of the medicine with him, and although another doctor from Indiana has come among us yet he has not the necessary medicines to cope with the diseases which [are] prostrating our men in this miserably dirty hole of secesh [secessionist] carrion and filth.

Saturday, February 8, 1862

Dull and cloudy today.

Having heard of the existence of a cave not far from our camp, I with H. Swift, W. B. Holton & A. Campbell of our company determine to go and see it today. Taking the road to Sommerset, [seat of Pulaski County, Kentucky,] we follow it to where it crosses the little stream which runs to the east of our camp, on a natural bridge, or rather where the stream loses itself beneath a perpendicular wall of rock some twenty feet high, above the road but emerges again from its rocky confinement some 250 yards below. A stranger passing the road would not know that he had crossed a stream. Turning off the road a little way, after some little trouble in searching we find a cave, and entering the mouth, light our candles, and proceed to explore and view the mysteries of this underground gallery.

Soon, [we] observe a light spot, find it is indeed a skylight, admitting the light of day into this subterranean vault, by a small hole overhead. Under this skylight lies a vast pile of stone and rubbish, amounting to hundreds of wagon loads, which has given away and [fallen] to the floor. As I looked at the pile of stone, dirt, etc. the thought crossed my mind, of some ponderous mythical wild beast of ancient days, having passed across overhead, and inadvertently stepping just over the cave with his large foot, broke the hole through. The mass of rock etc. which has broken loose give[s] the cave (which [is] here wide) or would give it, were the rubbish cleaned out, the appearance of a large vaulted room, with a lofty dome converging into the skylight at the top and center.

THE DIARY
FEBRUARY ENTRIES

Passing on we penetrate this underground passage to its termination, a distance of near a quarter of a mile; find much of curious interest to me; in many places the ceiling hung thick with rocky stalactites like pendant icicles to the eave[s] of the house in winter's frost, in other [places] they took the form and appearance of a beautiful drapery hung over the edge of a table, sometimes even resembling the drapery & loosely flowing robes of [a] marble statue. All of this was evidently formed by the dripping of the water for long ages, in which is infused mineral or other rocky substance, which gradually hardens with time and exposure to the air. Most of these rock icicles were hard and brittle but some of the smaller, and apparently more newly formed ones, were so soft as to be easily mashed between the thumb and finger. After gratifying our curiosities by a pretty thorough examination of the interior of this cave we emerge again from our subterranean explorations to the light of day.

On learning from some boys who had went [sic] with us into the cave that there was another cave some 1/2 mile distant which they called "our cave" and assured us that it was a prettier one than that we had just been in we concluded to visit it, guided by the boys. We soon reached the house or hovel where they lived and went in a moment at their invitation. I have seldom if ever seen a more poverty stricken looking place or family, but the old lady professed strong Union sentiments, and appeared not a little wrathful at some Union soldiers who she assured us had been there the night before to search her house and the cave for some rebels who had been seen the day before to leave an old coal boat on the river above us, and take to the brush. She was very anxious to trade anything she could spare for coffee. There are plenty of people hereabouts who would much rather have coffee for such things as they have to spare, (such as fowls, eggs, butter, milk, bread, etc.) than the gold. Leaving the house, we proceed to the cave along a plain beaten path.

On entering the mouth and just beyond the verge of daylight, I was surprised to see quite a strong spring of water issuing from the rock ceiling, and falling to a series of bowls or basins, and troughs formed in the rock, & I presume by the constant falling of the water, although

BY THE DIM AND FLARING LAMPS:
THE CIVIL WAR DIARY OF SAMUEL MCILVAINE

they had much the appearance of having been dressed out for the express purpose of receiving the water; and as if to complete the arrangements for a regular fountain, the rock which contained the troughs and basins was a large block of several tons weight, of square shape, and elevated in the center to the height of man's head or more, but with benches or shelves in which were scooped out the receptacles for the water. Here the family above alluded to get[ting] their water, having to take a light with them when going after water or grope in the dark for it.

We penetrated this cave to its extremity, even to getting down flat, and crawling into a place where there was an unusual quantity of beautiful stalactites. Found (as the boys had told us) this cave even more interesting than the first, and returned to the light of day much gratified with our underground explorations, richly repaid for our time and trouble.

These caves are known around here as "The Saltpeter Caves" and we saw the hoppers, troughs and other apparatus for its manufacture, together with large amounts of clay which had been leeched, as well as that which was not.

Saltpeter (sodium or potassium nitrate) is a by-product of bat and bird guano, plentiful in caves. Until the development of the Haber nitrogen fixation process during World War I, leeching guano was a major source of nitrates for explosives and fertilizer.

Passing back toward camp on the east side the ravine, we passed the rebel picket stands, and what appeared to have been a large cavalry camp. Passed a large field of wheat apparently destroyed by running over it with horses, wagons, etc.

On arriving at the camp just occupied by the 10th Kentucky they inform us that they have order[s] for immediately crossing back to the other side of the river again; they have hardly fairly got moved to this side yet.

On reaching camp we learn it is the turn of our company to go on picket tonight, therefore we get ready and start. I go with a squad to guard the road down river. Passing out half mile or more, [we] select a place for a good lookout near an old blacksmith's shop and stable, which affords us a good place for sleeping while not on the watch. I find an excellent place in the stable loft, on some unshucked corn.

Sunday, February 9, 1862

A little cool last night. The night passes off without any alarm or other incident worthy of note. The weather very fine and mild today.

Coming in off picket we learn we are to move back to the other side [of] the river, according[ly] all hands, at least all who are able, set to work. Everything has to be carried down the long steep hill to the river and then we have to wait the turn of our company, then ferry all over, pulling the boats over by means of a cable stretched across the river, then all [of us are] to carry up an almost perpendicular bluff of 100 feet high or upwards. I assisted in carrying the things to river, helped ferry all over, and carried several heavy loads up the steep bluff and to camp, but on reaching our old shanties found the teamsters had made stables of them. Here, then, is a new trouble, but after some little trouble we succeeded in finding a vacant cabin for our mess and the balance of the company scatter about in different places as they could find shanties, although most of the regiment have got moved back with their camp equipage, yet the sick are left on the other side as yet.

Monday, February 10, 1862

Froze pretty hard last night, but a very fine day succeeds, [and] soon thaws all it froze.

Arrangements are made this morning to move the sick over. A great many have to be carried in litters down to the river. Hereafter crossing arrangements are made to haul most of them up the hill, but

BY THE DIM AND FLARING LAMPS:
THE CIVIL WAR DIARY OF SAMUEL MCILVAINE

some are too sick to be drawn in a wagon and consequently have to be carried a long way around to get up the hill.

Of these is Thomas M. Cook of our mess. Cook has become much worse within the last day or two. I sit up with him tonight, to wait on him and give medicine until two or three o'clock A.M. It seemed useless to give any more medicine, and I never felt so loath to give medicine or anything else to a fellow creature, for it had to be forced down in great measure, often prying open his teeth to insert the spoon containing the medicine. It [became] evident that he could not live long.

Write considerable tonight (letters to friends). It was understood this evening that we were to start tomorrow morn for Sommerset. Arrangements were made and persons detailed to stay with and take care of the sick, who were to be left here. I thought it an exceedingly strange manner of doing business to go off and leave the sick in a deserted camp, where any roving band of the enemy might capture both them and their attendants, almost without medicine or medical [attendants], and especially in such an outrageously filthy place as this; and wondered why some arrangement had not been made to remove them to Sommerset in advance of us, but found no satisfactory response to my queries on this subject. Among the sick was our orderly sergeant.

Tuesday, February 11, 1862

Quite a snowstorm this morning, snowing and blowing when I get up, in what appeared to me quite the old fashioned style, and continue[s] for some time, and I began to wonder whether our officers would not postpone our departure, as it looked rather uninviting to leave our cabins and comfortable fires (the rebels had left us plenty of wood ready drawn to the doors) and turn out on a march in the storm. But preparations are making, and I learn we shall start storm or no storm. However before we get ready to start it ceases to snow and gets pleasant, and long ere night the snow had all disappeared.

THE DIARY
FEBRUARY ENTRIES

Around ten or eleven o'clock A.M. we leave this miserably dirty filthy rebel encampment, without any regrets on my part, except that our sick had to be left there. [Thomas M.] Cook is worse if possible this morning, and I learn our orderly is very bad. After our things are all loaded I essay [attempt] to hunt up the cabin where [he] was, to see and take leave of him, but not knowing where it was and no one to direct me, I fail after a considerable search to find him, and have to [give] it up, without seeing him. I had little idea then, that I never was to see him again.

The wagons had got some distance ahead, and I had considerable [part] of a load ... which I wished to put on the wagon, and therefore had to hasten on. We passed out over the same road we came on (where we chased the rebels to their camp), for several miles & turned off on [it] to visit or examine it. [I] had hopes we would march past it, but [I] was disappointed. Had I known in time what I afterward learned, that three or four of our company started in advance and went [to] it, I should have tried hard to be with them.

Crossed Fishing Creek this evening. Many of the men waded it, nearly to their waists, a good many we [carried] over on the officers' horses. A small canoe was also brought into requisition. As I was with the wagon I got an opportunity to ride over on it. [We] camp in a wood where there was plenty of good firewood.

William Holton and H. Swift, of our company, were quite unwell, and I had observed that they were nearly wearied out when I last passed them, and fearing they would not get into camp I got Capt. [either Joseph F. or Marsh B.] Taylor's horse and went back after them. This is the first time I have straddled a horse since I left home. I hardly knew whether I would be able to stick on, but it came as natural as eating, almost.

The country passed over today was mostly broken, and very poor soil, yet there was once in a while a poor looking house and farm, the timber poor and scrubby.

BY THE DIM AND FLARING LAMPS:
THE CIVIL WAR DIARY OF SAMUEL MCILVAINE

Wednesday, February 12, 1862

Very fine day. Start early, arrive at and pass through Sommerset; about eleven o'clock A.M. Camp a short distance north; on our way today passed an elevated knoll near the base of which Col. [William A.] Hoskins, as I learn, of the Kentucky 12th [Infantry], had thrown up earthworks, about the time Zollicoffer came in here. Most of the country passed today was much better than any we have seen lately. Passed one place where some enterprising farmer had gathered the stone[s] off his field, and converted them in[to] fence making a string 1/2 a mile long.

Sommerset is a small town, all wooden buildings. It has a desolate and forlorn look and appears as we pass through as if almost every other house were a hospital. I learn there are, and have been, a great many sick here, I presume sent from points east of here, and in addition to these, Gen. Schoepf has been here for some time with his command watching the rebels and holding them in check, and this place has become a point of rendezvous and a military station for stores of supplies, etc.

The whole country around here betokens the presence of armies and grim visaged war, hardly a fence is left around any of the fields, and many fine looking wheatfields are turned out to the commons.

On getting to camp, although I feel very tired and weary with wading through the mud, (for the roads are awful muddy) it is necessary to have water to cook with as well as to quench thirst. I take a bucket and start to hunt water but have to go through the mud clear back into town, (near a mile) before I find any; we afterward find an excellent spring issuing from a cavernous rock recess, and forming quite a branch as it flows off. We take advantage of this spring this evening to take a general bathing, many washing their clothes. Although quite a distance from camp, it is a most beautiful place for washing, bathing, etc.

Get the use of the shoe tools belonging to, or used by, T. F. S. Bennet, of our company (left at Campbellsville [seat of Taylor County,

Kentucky] sick) and put a half sole on one of my boots tonight, using a piece of secesh saddle skirt.

Thursday, February 13, 1862

Strike tents, pack up, and start before daylight this morn, our destination being Lebanon, Kentucky. The day becomes very fine; find the roads very bad and terribly cut up from the continued passing of heavy army wagons in drawing supplies to Sommerset. The country generally very poor, with shabby looking houses and farms, timber mainly black and white oak with an occasional chestnut ridge.

Friday, February 14, 1862

Rained last night, and turned to snow before day. Continued quite cool all day. When we strike our tents this morn and go to fold them up, find them stiff with snow and ice, and very difficult to fold up.

Continue our march today, passing over miles of recently constructed corduroy roads. These have been made of small trees cut and split, of pole, and occasionally of fence rails, by Union soldiers; these road continue for miles, in some places, over hills and hollows alike where it would be impossible almost, to get through the soft miry clay without them.

Camp this evening in a corn field. [We] have to scrape the snow off the ground to spread our tents. This leaves the soft plowed ground damp and cold. No straw is to be had (none at least in convenient reach). We make shift, however, to prevent laying on the damp ground by peeling chestnut bark. The trees being dead, the bark is easily obtained in large pieces.

BY THE DIM AND FLARING LAMPS:
THE CIVIL WAR DIARY OF SAMUEL MCILVAINE

Saturday, February 15, 1862

Quite cold and winter-like today.

Continue our march today. The country gradually as we pass through becomes better, although the roads get but little better until we strike the end of the pike, leading in this direction from Danville [seat of Boyle County, Kentucky], which we do about noon. From here forward, we have no more trouble with the roads; but before this [point], ... many farmers had reason to regret the difficulty of navigating the roads as [much] as ourselves. Numerous were the fields whose fences were thrown down, and whose soft loose soil was plowed up to the depth of two or more feet by the heavy army wagons of "Uncle Sam". It mattered little how valuable a crop the field might contain, if it but indicated a better passage for the wagons than the roads.

This morn [Lt.] Col. [William C.] Kise, William C. [10th Indiana Infantry] asked Lt. Van Natta if he wanted a recruit, saying a stout hearty looking man had applied to be admitted to the 10th Regiment, had been in the Mexican war, was an Indianian, and had traveled a long way, purposely to join our regiment. He was sworn into the service as a member of our company, his name Charles Bowling.

We pass Hall's Gap in the range of hills known as Muldrow's. This range of hills it would seem is quite extensive, as we were near them when at the Rolling Fork Salt River, and [we cross] them ... again ... through this gap.

Quite a pleasant prospect opens to our view, as we wind around the point of the hill and down the pike into an open country. A great change for the better in both soil, agricultural improvements and general thrift & wealth. As we approach and pass through Stanford [seat of Lincoln County, Kentucky], the country continues to improve, and is the finest of any I have seen in this State. In fact, we have been passing for so long through such poverty stricken country that I almost began to doubt the truth of a good and fine country in Kentucky.

Pass through Stanford this evening and camp a little way from town, find the snow much deeper here than where we camped last night. Here again we have to shovel off the snow to make our beds, but fortunately the country here is able to furnish us with plenty of straw.

Sunday, February 16, 1862

Froze quite sharp last night, reminding us of home in the winter.
Remain in camp today for the purpose of getting the horses and mules reshod, writing, etc. Made a visit to the town today. It is a small town, but a rather pleasant looking place when compared with any we have seen of late. [We] are visited in camp today by numerous citizens and among them this eve by several quite sprightly young ladies. They were entertained by some of our musical soldiers with patriotic songs accompanied by instrumental performance, after which Col. Manson proposed to show them through camp, that they might see how the boys lived. This he [did] in quite a humorous style.

Col. (later Brig. Gen.) Mahlon Dickerson Manson (1820-95) commanded the 2nd Brigade, of which the Indiana 10th was a part. After the war, he was elected to the House of Representatives.[3]

Monday, February 17, 1862

Strike tents early this morn and start in the rain which continued with little intermission all day. Cross west fork [of] Dick's River on a good bridge. This is one of the upper and western tributaries of the Kentucky River.

We pass through Danville this evening, county seat of Boyle County, a very handsome place, much the best built, largest and most business looking place we have seen since we passed through Louisville

---
3 Boatner, p. 508.

BY THE DIM AND FLARING LAMPS:
THE CIVIL WAR DIARY OF SAMUEL MCILVAINE

on our first advent into the State. It is also surrounded by much the finest country we have passed through in the State. It would seem we have come into the edge of the bluegrass region, which is the garden of the State; the country is indeed a beautiful one, beautiful clover fields and bluegrass pastures, with extensive fields of beautiful green wheat, have here taken the place of the little rocky, clayey, hilly & stumpy fields, presenting nothing but their bald, clayey faces (except occasionally a small patch of wheat). Splendid residences take the place of the log huts we have so long been greeted with, large and convenient barns take the place of the little pole or rail stable; the people wear a look of intelligence and manhood; even the fair sex become more fair; in short everything indicates that it would be a pleasant country to live in.

As we pass through we often pass lengthy strings of stone wall along the lanes. There is also much Bostand rail fence, the latter reminding me vividly of the times when greeted with the presence of her fair daughters, the waving of flags and cheering of the populace. Here we turn west toward Lebanon, [Kentucky] passing (a little out of town) the very pleasant residence of Col. Fry who just now is the subject of many congratulations and ovations, and in fact has become quite a noted person, as to him is accredited the honor (or glory if you choose) of shooting the rebel Gen. Zollicoffer.

I stopped this eve at a house near the road to try to get some milk for one of the boy[s], who was unwell and had fallen behind. The lady of the house was exceedingly friendly and talkative. [She] plied me with a great many questions in regard to the army, the battle, etc. insomuch that I found it difficult to get away. It was buttermilk I wanted. She had given that all away, but gave me some sweet milk, and cited me to the next neighbor where she thought I could get plenty. I called at this house, where they were just sitting down to a late dinner. Here I found another expression of friendship to the soldiers in an urgent solicitation to stay and eat with them although two or three soldiers were already at the table. I concluded to avail myself of the good lady's hospitality, although at the risk of getting far behind the regiment. They had cider at table, which I thought the best beverage I had tasted since leaving home.

THE DIARY
FEBRUARY ENTRIES

We camped this eve in a beautiful wood pasture about five miles west of Danville. We had heard through the day rumors of the taking of Fort Donaldson [Donelson]. This evening a bulletin was brought into camp fully confirming the rumor.

Fort Donelson, on the Cumberland River, was taken by Union forces under the command of Gen. Grant and Flag Officer Foote after a battle lasting from February 12-16. Fort Donelson (and its neighbor, Fort Henry) blocked the most natural invasion routes along the Tennessee and Cumberland Rivers. This victory by Grant's troops marked the beginning of Grant's rise to prominence.[4]

Gen. Grant's famous "Unconditional Surrender" message was given at Fort Donelson in response to Confederate Gen. Simon B. Buckner's request for surrender terms.[5]

Tuesday, February 18, 1862

Cloudy and gloomy today. Strike our tents and start at daylight.

I forgot to mention in yesterday's proceedings that [we] were followed to camp by three or four slave hunters. They were admitted into the camp and soon found their runaway slaves. They had come in at Danville, [Kentucky,] got mixed with the Negro cooks and waiters and were thus endeavoring [to] effect their escape to the North. There were two of them, one had armed himself with a pistol, the other with a butcher knife; they had evidently counted on being protected in the regiment but [they] were sadly disappointed, as they were disarmed by their pursuers and taken back without molestation on our part.

---

[4] Boatner, pp. 394-397.
[5] Boatner, p. 857.

BY THE DIM AND FLARING LAMPS:
THE CIVIL WAR DIARY OF SAMUEL MCILVAINE

The Emancipation Proclamation was still in the future, and President Lincoln, concerned about angering slaveholders in the border states that had remained loyal to the Union, had ordered Union officers to return runaway slaves to their masters.

> We passed through Perrysville [Perryville, Kentucky]. This is a small town, but I noticed a very fine building just before entering town, which was used as an academy or college for young ladies. They came out to the road to see the regiment pass and were a fine looking set of girls. The country still continued good; and as we pass numerous old orchards, I try to get a canteenful of cider to drink while on the march with my hard bread, but fail to find any more. Camp this evening in a fine old woods and near a sugar orchard, [the] ground wet and damp but find sufficiency of straw for beds.

The "sugar orchard" probably refers to sugar beets.
Hard bread, also called "hardtack" in the Army of the Potomac, was a hard biscuit commonly issued as a marching ration. Soldiers ate it in a variety of ways: broken in coffee, spoiled, and with maggots. Contemporary accounts suggest it was not popular.[6]

Wednesday February 19, 1862

> Raining this morning, rained all day and in the evening very hard.
> Strike tents early and arrive at Lebanon [Kentucky] about noon. Country not so good today, more rolling and broken, with thin soil, very disagreeable marching today through the mud, slop and rain. As we pass through town, I (being with the wagons, as I have been all the

---
6 Billings, pp. 112-119.

way through from Mill Spring), stop a moment at the Post Office, and on starting again go straight forward toward our old camp, but soon find they have not gone this way. The regiment had passed out of sight and among the multiplicity of army wagons going in all directions find myself much put to it to get the course. In hunting around find Swift of our company (who be[ing] unwell had fallen behind) also lost as to the track they had taken. We however by enquiry finally get the course and find the regiment encamped about 1 1/2 miles out on the Bardstown pike.

The ground where our tents were to be pitched was a sluice of mud and water and although I feel more wearied than I have any day since entering the service, it seemed absolutely necessary to have something dry to lay on. Therefore as the rain had slacked a little and gave, as I thought, indication of clearing off, [I] started to hunt straw. [I heard] of none anywhere near [at first]; but finally got track of some and go ... fully a mile before I find it. Soon after starting [it] commenced raining again. [I] had left my oilcloth at camp. Arriving at the straw, find it a pile mostly rotten or spoiled. After much exertion and pulling straw by small handfuls in a shower of rain which increases every moment, finally succeed in getting a fair sized bundle of tolerably passable straw and putting it on my shoulders to shield ... the rain as much as possible. Return to camp through a pouring shower of rain, getting perfectly soaked.

Although we use a neighboring string of fence for fuel and to make bed of, we find it very difficult to cook anything, and are obliged to stay our hunger [from] our hard march, with such cold scraps as we can best get hold of without hard crackers [hard bread].

On examination I find my writing material, including some books, and my diary or journal, some underclothing and various little notions in my carpet-sack, about as thoroughly water soaked as myself; the carpet-sack was in the wagon, on which there was no cover.

... I might have put my knapsack on the wagon (as most of the others did), ... especially as I was with the wagon all the time, yet I preferred carrying it, including my overcoat & blanket (under cover of my oilcloth), to prevent their getting wet. We finally as night approached

BY THE DIM AND FLARING LAMPS:
THE CIVIL WAR DIARY OF SAMUEL MCILVAINE

get tolerably comfortably situated for the night, although I lay down with my clothes still saturated with water. I was much wearied tonight, and found this the hardest day I have experienced in the army.

Thursday, February 20, 1862

Gloomy and cloudy today. Froze a little last night. Move our camp about a mile further east, to a better situation. We here find plenty of wood and dry straw convenient. Spend most of the day in drying my things and myself, or rather my clothing by a good fire, write some etc.

Am agreeably surprised to see Lt. Sappington [and] James Godman of our company make their appearance in camp today; they had been left here sick when our regiment left here for Mill Spring. We had been so long separated I had almost forgotten them.

The day is spent in resting, drying clothing, cleaning up arms, etc. Some clothing was also distributed and most of the regiment got pants of a sky blue.

A rumor in camp that the government of Tennessee had ordered the State Militia to lay down their arms. This is received as joyful news.

Friday, February 21, 1862

Gloomy and cloudy, with more or less rain today.

William Holton of [our] company failed to come in last eve; it is learned that he is at old Mr. Bell's near town and is sick.

Remain in camp. Nothing of particular importance transpires in camp. I spend the time in writing, reading etc., get papers today giving the particulars of the taking of Fort Donaldson [Donelson], and much other good news.

THE DIARY
FEBRUARY ENTRIES

Saturday, February 22, 1862

Rains nearly all day. Some talk yesterday eve [and] this morning of striking tents, but as it sets in to raining, if it [a move] was *really* intended, probably a move was postponed on account of the rain. Notwithstanding, the boys have a song which commences, "Never strike tents unless it is raining".

Remain in camp today; read, write to friends, etc. Some firing of cannon today, in the vicinity of Lebanon [Kentucky] in honor of Washington's birthday. If it were possible that the spirit of the great and good Washington could revisit the scenes of his Earthly labor, how must it mourn over the unhappy and distracted condition of this once peaceful and happy country.

Sunday, February 23, 1862

Quite pleasant today.

Guards having again been put on for the last day or two, it came my turn to go on guard today. Spend the time when not on guard in writing, reading the news, which continues of the most glorious nature for our cause.

Our chaplain [Rev. George T. Dougherty] seems to have entirely forgot or discarded his duties. If I mistake not, he has never preached to us since we left here for Mill Spring and even some time previously.

Monday, February 24, 1862

March this morning for Bardstown. William Holton, Charles Baker and perhaps one or two others of our company left here sick.

We have an excellent pike and make good time. Blusters some this morning and rains a little yet it is ... cool and pleasant marching. Pass through Springfield, county seat of Washington County, a small town. Pass some very good farming country but face of the [land] becomes

BY THE DIM AND FLARING LAMPS:
THE CIVIL WAR DIARY OF SAMUEL MCILVAINE

more broken. Cross Cots Creek, [a] small stream. Pass through Fredericksburgh, [a] very small place. Cross considerable branch of Rolling Fork Salt River; country becomes more broken and hilly. No bodies of heavy timber. Camp within five miles of Bardstown on the rocky bank of a babbling brook, having marched some twenty miles or more.

Tuesday, February 25, 1862

Moderately cool today.

Start early; soon reach Bardstown; approaching it through a very rough, broken, and rocky, country. The people seem to receive [us] as old friends, and with lively demonstrations of pleasure. The populace (where we were camped so long) the people and associations, do indeed look familiar & bring back a recollection of many pleasant scenes. The people desirous to testify their good will toward us, greet us with cheers, as the "heroes of Mill Spring" and even bring out liquor and treat the whole regiment. The ladies receive us with smiles, waving of handkerchiefs, flags, and other testimonies of pleasure and respect. Many glances are exchanged, and many hasty enquiries made between our sturdy boys and the *fair* denizens of the town during our brief stop in the streets.

Our regiment are drawn up in front of the hospital, and after a few brief remarks by Col. Manson, three cheers were given for Indiana sick soldiers here, and we resumed our march, taking the pike for Louisville. We found here the Michigan 11th Regiment and learned they had been here since soon after we left last fall, kept here, I presume, in consequence of being infected by contagious disease.

As I pass through the streets, one of our men calls my attention to a young soldier he was conversing with, and to my surprise I discovered him to be one of my near neighbor boys, R. Stokes who had enlisted since I left home in the 10th Indiana. He had been left here sick, had as he assured me came very near dying. He was so emaciated I should not have known him had not my attention been especially called to him; [I] had but little time to tarry with him as the regiment was moving on.

So we pass out of town [and] get a fine view of our old camping and drill grounds across the ravine in Gov. Wickliffe's Meadow, now being plowed up, but made classic by the publication of a poem alluding to it in the New York Tribune.

How fleeting is fame. I was unable to find any information concerning Gov. Wickliffe, his meadow, or the poem published in the New York Tribune.

Passing out by the graveyard, I enter it to look at the graves of the two men we left here and [I am] much surprised to find a large scope of ground covered over with soldiers' graves. [Ah, full [with] many a poor fellow who, burning with patriotism, shouldered his musket and rushed forth in all the blooming health and strength of youth, to defend the institutions of his fathers and his country, has here found an untimely grave, far from home and friends, even before he was permitted to meet his country's foes.] The graves of the Indiana soldiers occupy a corner of the graveyard, and a numerous array of little freshly made mounds testify to the number of her brave sons who have been gently laid in their lowly resting places here by their comrades, since we left here.

Three out of five Union fatalities were the result of disease, not hostile action.[7]

Passing on through a rather broken country, but on an excellent pike, we cross Salt River late this evening and camp in a little strip of meadow about two miles north of the river, have made another heavy day's march and are all very tired.

---

7 Stewart Brooks, *Civil War Medicine*, (Springfield, IL: Charles C. Thomas Publishers, 1966), p. 6.

BY THE DIM AND FLARING LAMPS:
THE CIVIL WAR DIARY OF SAMUEL MCILVAINE

It has transpired to the regiment that Col. Manson and Lt. Col. Kise have been put under arrest by their superiors, but for what is not definitely understood, hence the command of the regiment has devolved upon Major [A.O.] Miller for some time past. Since we have been making such heavy marches many of the boys are disposed to curse the major for trying to run them to death. ... I am much more inclined to think we are indebted for our heavy marching either to an imperative order to be at Louisville at a certain date, or else to an animosity which seems to have arisen somehow between our regiment and the 14th Ohio, ... which seems to be making itself felt by a trial of bottom of the respective regiments. Our camp is some two or three miles in advance of the 14th this evening, they having the lead today.

"Trial of bottom" is a most picturesque expression; from the context it seems to refer to the two regiments competing in marching speed.

Wednesday, February 26, 1862

It was whispered around slyly last evening that we were to take a very early start this morning in order to keep ahead of the Ohio 14th and it was even said that a picket was stationed near enough to their camp to be cognizant of their movement this morn, and who was to give notice thereof by firing his piece. Accordingly about twelve or one o'clock [A.M.], we were aroused and, hastily getting breakfast [we] struck tents, loaded up, had barely got the regiment formed and onto the road, when the 14th came up, even before our teams got onto the road. They shoved on and soon overtaking our men mixed in with them; it was misting rain and exceedingly dark.

Soon a wordy strife commenced, which threatened to culminate in blows, (it is said one of the Ohio men was so unthoughted [unthinking], as to throw up "Buena Vista" to our men, and immediately got knocked down for it). Their colonel (Steadman [Steedman]), seeing a difficulty

was brewing, and that we clearly had the road, halted his men. Ours going on arrived at Louisville an hour or two in advance of them. It would seem that the Ohio 14th failing (in consequence of being sent out on a scout) to get a chance to participate in the battle near Mill Spring, being in the same brigade with us, and perhaps somewhat chagrined over this affair, concluded to prove to the world that they could at least, beat us in marching by getting to Louisville first; but even in this they were thwarted.

"Buena Vista" refers to the ill-timed, and apparently cowardly retreat of the Indiana 2nd Regiment at the Battle of Buena Vista during the Mexican War.[8]

It was a marvel to me how we got along with the teams this exceedingly dark and misty morn without running off the pike or oversetting [overturning] numberless time[s]; yet we passed along without accident or incident, so far as I know, (and I was with the teams) down and up hills, around short curves, etc. making very nearly half the distance to Louisville, (a distance of over twenty miles) by sunup.

We passed through the little village of Mount Washington [Bullitt County, Kentucky], soon after starting apparently without arousing a solitary individual; notwithstanding the passing of our whole regiment and the rumbling of our wagons, not a light was perceptible. I saw one large and apparently good building at the side of the street which I took for a church-house; this is all I can say of *this* place.

As we approach Louisville the country changes and loses its hilly and rugged appearance and becomes quite level and as it is highly cultivated the landscape is a very pleasant one. Passed many very fine farms and handsome residences, and near the city, the land seems to have been nearly all converted into gardens. The landscape is very different on this approach to the city, to that lying along the Southern Railway, on which we passed out of it. We arrived in the suburbs of

---

8 John Edward Weems, *To Conquer A Peace*, (Garden City, NY: Doubleday & Co., 1974), p. 304.

BY THE DIM AND FLARING LAMPS:
THE CIVIL WAR DIARY OF SAMUEL MCILVAINE

the city about eleven o'clock A.M. Having traveled about 22 miles this morning, [we] pitch our tents on a rising ground south of the city, and seek the rest our weary bodies need after our rapid march.

It is not long until the fact of our return is known in the city, and there is quite a visiting kept up by the citizen[s] both male and female [till that] night. Many of the fair daughters of Louisville visit us, and mingle in social chat with officers and men, and among them Misses Sallie Mansfield & Betty Craft, who presented us a splendid flag last fall, as a token of gratitude to us for the promptness with which we rushed to the rescue when Louisville was threatened by Buckner's traitorous band, and they now have another to present us as we march through their city, in appreciation of our bravery at Mill Spring.

Brig. Gen. Simon Bolivar Buckner (1823-1914): At the beginning of the war, Buckner attempted to keep Kentucky neutral.[9] When Kentucky required State Guard officers to take a Union loyalty oath, he joined the Confederate Army as a brigadier general, taking many members of the State Guard with him.[10] Buckner reinforced Fort Donelson, while the senior Confederate generals escaped, leaving Buckner to surrender the fort to Gen. Grant. Buckner later returned to Confederate service as a result of a prisoner exchange.

Samuel treats Buckner much more harshly than his enemies did. Buckner was so respected by Gen. Grant that he served as a pallbearer at Grant's funeral. Buckner was governor of Kentucky from 1887-1892, and the Vice

---

[9] Boatner, pp. 95-96.
[10] Allan Nevins, *War For The Union*, (Charles Scribner's Sons, 1959), I, 134-135.

Presidential nominee of the National (Gold) Democratic Party in 1896.[11]

Buckner's son, Lt. Gen. Simon Bolivar Buckner, Jr., commanded the U.S. invasion of the Ryukyu Islands during World War II.[12]

Thursday, February 27, 1862
Louisville

Froze pretty sharp last night; but soon gets pleasant.

Strike tents this morning, [march through the city, with music and colors flying, greeted by throngs of people at every corner with flags, and handkerchiefs waving, everything indicating that the loyal citizens view us as conquering heroes.] I was with the wagons, and unable to witness the demonstrations as well as if I had been in the ranks; but as an instance of their good will toward us, I may mention [an] instance that occurred to myself. As I passed along the sidewalk, I was hailed by a lady from an upper window, desiring to know if I did not want a good pair of woolen gloves (I *suppose* she noticed me bare handed) at the same time motioning to throw them to me. I assured her I had a good pair & passed on. As I turned towards the wagons one of our sick men (John Scott) called to me to get them for him. The lady hearing him, immediately tossed them to me.

Passing down through the city (which as observed when passing through last fall, is very compactly built) near the river the regiment is halted in [the] street & standing in column are presented with the aforementioned flag, as a testimonial to our firmness and bravery at Mill Spring against a greatly superior force of the enemy. It contained the following inscription:

---

[11] Boatner, p. 96.
[12] "Buckner, Simon Bolivar, Jr.", *Encyclopedia Brittanica*, 1983, Micropaedia II, pp. 340-341.

BY THE DIM AND FLARING LAMPS:
THE CIVIL WAR DIARY OF SAMUEL MCILVAINE

Mill Spring   January 19th 1862,
Presented to the Indiana 10th Regiment
By the Loyal Ladies of Louisville, Kentucky

The 9th Ohio, 2nd Minnesota, and 4th Kentucky each received a similar flag, and for the same reasons.

After this ceremony was through, our regiment marched down to the wharf and went aboard the steamers *Glendale* and *Lady Pike*, and proceeded to take on the teams and wagons, the latter being taken apart and stowed in the hold, and all our camp equipage, which was also mostly stowed in the hold. A large quantity of forage and commissary stores was also taken on board, numerous other steamers were also lying at the wharf receiving a similar lading of troops and supplies; the streets were literally crowded with army wagons and the city seemed full of soldiers.

It was now I got my first *good* view of the noble Ohio, flowing in all its majesty, as it did when the Red Man alone stood upon its banks, or paddled his bark canoe swiftly over its glassy surface. It flows swiftly on, (now much swollen) in its turbid and mad course, as if conscious of its mighty power; and ready alike to bear onward to their destination thousands of men with all the paraphernalia of war and destruction, or the generous fruits of the soil, and all the peaceful commodities of a noble and hitherto uninterrupted commerce. Ah, noble old river! could thee but speak, what tales of horror thou couldst unfold; of blood, of murder, of steamboat collisions, of bursting boilers, of burnings, scaldings and drowning men and women and children.

Availing myself of the opportunity while the lading [loading] of the boats is going on, take the secesh rifle I captured at the rebel encampment (and which I have succeeded in bringing with me so far), my secesh blanket, and saddlebags, and the bed comfort[er] which the noble Mrs. Gillman gave me, my diary or journal (brought up to the 5th ...) my letters, etc. carry them to the express office, fix them up in a package, and express them home, in care H. T. Sample at Lafayette, [Indiana]. [I] address a short note to James McConnell & Barns at

THE DIARY
FEBRUARY ENTRIES

Oxford [Benton County, Indiana, asking them to] get them from Lafayette & convey them to my wife, enclosing the expressmen's receipt.

Samuel's diary "brought up to the 5th" would immediately precede this diary, the first entry of which is dated February 5th. This previous diary has not been passed through my branch of the family.

By dark or soon after, our equipage and stores are all aboard, and we retire to rest, expecting the boat soon to start. The cabin floor and galleries running outside the cabin are literally covered with sleeping soldiers crowded so close that it is almost impossible to pass among them with[out] stepping upon some sleeper's foot or hand. Our company occupy one of the side galleries tonight and some of them even sleep upon the hurricane [promenade] deck. We leave in hospital H. Swift, J. M. Adwell, and several others of our company and many of the regiment.

Friday, February 28, 1862

Cool and frosty last night. On awakening this morning find [our] boat the *Glendale* moored at the wharf. Something has detained her all night. The *Lady Pike*, with the left wing of our regiment, had shoved off in the night.

Soon after sunup, our boat shoves off and turning her prow downstream, we soon leave the commercial metropolis of Kentucky behind. Although some of our officers may have learned ere this where we were bound to, yet few of the men had any idea of our destination, and I freely admit, that I knew not until we shoved off from the wharf, whether we were going up or down the river ... It began to be understood soon after starting that we were destined to Nashville, Tennessee (Gen. Buell finding it more convenient to move that part of his army at

BY THE DIM AND FLARING LAMPS:
THE CIVIL WAR DIARY OF SAMUEL MCILVAINE

Mill Spring and Sommerset back to Louisville, down the Ohio, and up the Cumberland to Nashville, than to undertake to draw subsistence for them, while they should march there, across the country). Indeed it would have been an almost impossible thing to do in the present condition of the roads.

Although Capt. Taylor of our company had told me before leaving Mill Spring that he had tendered his resignation, to take effect the 1st [of] March, (alleging therefore his age and inability to withstand the hardship of camp life) and had expected to get his papers fixed by this time and go from here home, yet on arriving here found that Gen. Buell had moved his headquarters to Nashville. He was perforce constrained to go with us there.

A little clump of trees with a very small *perceivable* patch of soil about their roots are standing in the midst of the river a little way below where our boat lay. I know not but think it probable this is the island (now covered by water by the high stage of the river) alluded to in the history of the first settlement of Louisville, now nearly a century ago, as the island where the first settlers of Louisville took refuge from the Indians for a season and whence they emerged to found the city.

As we leave the landing and move off down the river, the city is seen to stretch far down the bank, finally dwindling away into a few scattering houses; whilst Jeffersonville makes a fine display on the opposite bank, the Capitol house for the "lower class" *assembly* of the State of Indiana (penitentiary) occupying a conspicuous position at the lower edge of the city, with its extensive *pleasure grounds* fenced in with a high stone wall.

New Albany in Indiana is also in sight but a little way below, and as it glitters in the morning sun looks like a snug little village perched upon a high bank; yet as we approach closer its dimensions seem to increase somewhat, yet it looks like a small city compared with my previous ideas of it. It is situated at a very short curve in the river and on a high bank which perhaps hides a good portion of it from the view from the river. It is the county seat of Floyd County.

It would seem hardly necessary to speak of the towns and scenery along this well known river; yet as these jottings may fall into the

THE DIARY
FEBRUARY ENTRIES

hands of some who like myself have but a poor idea of the views along this river, I will devote a few lines to a brief description. As we pass rapidly down we soon pass the mouth of the Salt River. A very small town is here, called Westport [West Point, Hardin County, Kentucky]. [Here] we also find a camp of Union soldiers with fortifications thrown up.

As we pass this camp, I am for the first time greeted with music by steam. A stream of deep toned, loud, sonorous, and wild shrieking music, which may be heard for miles, is pealed forth. *Steam* (what will it not be made to do yet) is made to perform the national air "Hail, Columbia", "Yankee Doodle", "Dixie", etc. with a precision I had not dreamed of. The instrument from which it issues (the calliope) is located upon the hurricane deck, and is operated like a melodian or accordian by thumb, or finger pieces.

We next pass Brandensburgh [Brandenburg], county seat of Meade County, Kentucky, a smart little town. Next, Newamsterdam in Indiana, quite small, although the county seat of Crawford County. Next village ... is Boonsport and Concordia in Kentucky and Derby in Indiana, all quite small places. Rome on the Indiana side is a smart sized town, and county seat of Perry County. Stepensport [Stephensport] immediately opposite in Kentucky is quite small. Next, at a short curve of the river, and situated on high ground, is Cloverport & Thompsonville on Kentucky side, all apparently constituting but one town and not very large at that, but there is a railroad pointing out into the country a short distance from here.

The next town we reach is Canelton [Cannellton], on Indiana side. It is principally situated on a kind of bench in the river bank, running back some distance to the more elevated ground, and is a smart sized town. It is in the vicinity of this place that the celebrated Canelton [Canellton] coalfields are located, and we stop here to take on coal for our trip. A track is laid from the water's edge [to] the coal mines, upon which cars for bringing in the coal are propelled by horse or mule power. This seems to be a general coaling point, and extensive arrangements are made for supplying it. A cotton factory was established here a number of years since by an Eastern company, under a

BY THE DIM AND FLARING LAMPS:
THE CIVIL WAR DIARY OF SAMUEL MCILVAINE

charter from the State Legislature; the building for which (a very fine large stone structure) stands conspicuous to the view near the river, but I could perceive very little signs of life about it.

Hawsville [Hawesville], immediately opposite in Kentucky and the county seat of Hancock County, is about the size of Canelton [Cannellton], and like it is also a coaling place.

Having taken on a good supply of coal, detaining for that purpose some three or four hours, we again start, soon passing on Kentucky side a small and quite new looking town called Tell City. Next is Maxville or Troy in Indiana, quite small, but nicely situated at the extremity of a considerable northward curve of the river. Next comes Lewisport on Kentucky side, small. Next is Rockport in Indiana, a considerable sized town and county seat of Spencer County.

Here it gets too dark to distinguish objects satisfactorily and I [go] to bed, if lying on the hard floor, with nothing under me but an oilcloth, and perchance a blanket, or an old bedquilt, and in one of the side galleries of a steamboat, may be called "going to bed". At Cannelton [Cannellton] and from there on down until it becomes [too] dark to see, the river seems to have become quite perceptibly wider than above.

About nine or ten o'clock I was awakened by the stopping of the boat. Curious to know what was going on, I got up and took the stairs to the hurricane deck, to avoid running over sleeping soldiers, [and] found we were moored at the wharf of what appears quite a considerable city. Large and tall blocks of buildings, apparently store & warehouse etc. fronted the river. Standing almost at the water's edge, during the very few moments we stopped here, I noticed from my perch upon the edge [of the] hurricane [deck], greetings and congratulations being exchanged by military officials, who have here met perhaps for the first in a considerable time. I should have liked much to have had a daylight view of the city.

March Entries

Saturday, March 1, 1862
Ohio River

It set in to raining during the night and became so dark we could not run with safety, and therefore [we] drew up to the bank and tied up to the trees. Learned to my great disappointment that we passed during the night the mouth of the Green and Wabash Rivers.

The Wabash River forms the boundary between Illinois and Indiana.

Although the morning is dark and rainy, the view is magnificent; the noble old Ohio, having received the waters of the Green and Wabash, has increased its size and volume in proportion, and presents to the view in its present high stage a grand sheet of water, much the largest I have ever seen, except on one occasion (that of [a] visit to Chicago, and [the] view of Lake Michigan).

Caseyville, a small town on the Kentucky side, is the first town of any note we pass this morning. Some other very small places are passed, among them Elizabethtown, county seat of Hardin County, Illinois and we pass Golconda, a very pretty little town, built on, or rather in, the side of the river's bluff, and county seat of Pope County, Illinois. Here we pass the first island I have seen except the one previously mentioned at Louisville, although we very probably passed others during the night. There is a farm with orchard and good buildings on it.

It has ceased to rain, and although pretty cool and windy, I cannot refrain from the inclination to indulge my curiosity, by remaining most of the time on the hurricane [promenade] deck. The scenery is grand, the Old River here flows in all his wonted strength and majesty, apparently near a mile in width, and bearing on his now riled and muddy

BY THE DIM AND FLARING LAMPS:
THE CIVIL WAR DIARY OF SAMUEL MCILVAINE

bosom large amounts of driftwood and not unfrequently washing away the fencing along the bottom and even passing his compliments with the inhabitants by walking unceremoniously into their doors. He is not particular even as to time; entering to the no small consternation of the inhabitants and stirring them up to a lively sense of his presence at midnight as likely as any other time.

We now frequently pass islands, generally small, and finally Smithland, situated on a tolerably high ground or bench of the river bluff and immediately at and below the mouth of the Cumberland River, looms up to our view. About eleven o'clock A.M. we touch at Smithland [Kentucky] but for a moment; this is comparatively a small, and quite an old and weather beaten looking place, the county seat of Livingston County, Kentucky. Here also are fortifications with mounted cannon, on a high bluff ... back of the town, so arranged as to command the Ohio as well as the mouth of the Cumberland. There is also [a] considerable encampment of Union troops here.

Opposite the mouth of the Cumberland is quite a considerable island, now nearly covered by water, but on which there is a house and appearances of a farm. There is a wide stretch of water here apparently near two miles in width; but here we turn into the mouth of the Cumberland, and take leave of the Ohio.

How very different is the navigation of the Ohio now, compared with that of 75 or 80 years ago! And how very different the scenery that greets the view. In those dangerous times, the hardy pioneer who first settled these vast and beautiful domains committed his worldly wealth and his family to the unwieldy flatbottomed boat, shoved it off into the stream to float with the current until he reached the destined point of debarkation, (if indeed he were permitted to pass unmolested by the wily Red Man). No beautiful villages, towns and cities, or farms, with growing grain and lowing herds greeted the view at every turn in the river... On the contrary, too often [he was] greeted at some abrupt turn by the sharp crack of the deadly rifle, the savage war whoop, and the sight of a fleet of Indian canoes filled with painted savages shoving direct for their boat, for the purpose of death & plunder. Then happy were they if by force of numbers, a sure and quick aim, aided by the protection of their boat, they were able to beat off their savage waylayers, and proceed upon their voyage.

Modern sensibilities are offended by this view of the Indians; certainly by the standards of the time, Samuel's perceptions of the Indians were not unusual.

But *now*, the immigrant, or other voyager upon the Ohio, steps onto one of the palatial steamers, which daily and nightly, ply up and down this river, and where he can be furnished with every desirable convenience & comfort, to say nothing of luxuries, which he can covet, all of which he enjoys at his leisure while proceeding rapidly on his journey. ... [T]he banks of the river, which used only to present to the lonely immigrant an unbroken forest, filled with wild beasts and savages ready to devour him, *now* presents on those same bank[s], at almost ever[y] turn, a fine farm or plantation in good state of cultivation with good dwelling and outhouses; a snug little hamlet or more stately city, with its large blocks of stone and brick warehouses and stores indicative alike of resources and prosperity of the country, while moored at the wharf are large numbers of steamboats loading and unloading the commodities of a magnificent commerce. Such are some of the changes which have taken place along this river within one short lifetime. But I must hasten from this digression.

We make but a moment's stop at the landing of Smithland, but turning into the mouth of the Cumberland proceed immediately up that river. It looks so narrow at the mouth, that it hardly appears as if it would receive our boat, but we soon find it gradually getting wider. We soon overtake and pass the *Lady Pike* with [the] left wing of our regiment the boys hallowing to, congratulating, and passing jokes with each other as we pass. Soon we begin to pass houses surrounded by water, fields and farms overflowed. [We] find this river even higher than the Ohio.

Pass Dyersburg [Dycusburg, Crittenden County, Kentucky], a very little place, and stop at [a] good-sized wood pile for two or three hours

BY THE DIM AND FLARING LAMPS:
THE CIVIL WAR DIARY OF SAMUEL MCILVAINE

to wood and shove forward again. The river *here* has overflowed the bottoms, which unlike those described far above at Mill Spring, are very wide and the banks low, and spreading out over the adjoining country, presents a vast sheet of water as far as we can see.

Pass this eve the steamer *Economy*, recently wrecked, (and now in sunken state) while passing up this river with troops and government stores. Some army wagons are yet standing near it which have been put ashore but now entirely surrounded by water for a mile distant.

Proceeding up we pass Eddyville, county seat of Lyon County, Kentucky. It is quite a small town. We finally heave to and tie up for the night, near a little town called Rockcastle, as it is unsafe to navigate this narrow river in the dark. Another steamer is here on its way down river from which we get considerable news in regard to matters in Nashville. [We] learn that Buell's army are in peaceable possession of the city or a part of it whilst the rest are daily arriving and being ferried over the river, but that little if any Union feeling is manifested in the city.

Sunday, March 2, 1862
Cumberland River

Start at daylight this morning.

Pass Canton [Trigg County, Kentucky], a small town. The river is exceedingly high, spreading out over the bottoms, through the woods and brush, over fields and fencing till it presents a sheet of water I should judge two miles in width, rising into houses and little towns, in some instances nearly submerging them, to the no little annoyance and discomfiture of the inmates. At many houses ... we see boats tied up ready in the last emergency to carry off the family and goods to higher ground; or in which some member of the family, after removing his friends and goods, has returned to see what is likely to become of the house.

Pass Tobaccoport [Stewart County], a very small town just after we cross the Tennessee line. River banks become more rocky and abrupt than heretofore. About eleven o'clock A.M. pass the severely and recently contested battlefield of Fort Donaldson [Donelson]. The fort, or batteries, occupy a high bluff bank and completely command the river. The cannon were [still] mounted. I had hoped we would be landed here for a few moments and permitted to mount the bank and take a view of the battlefield, but not so, we passed by without stopping. I had therefore to content myself with a very poor view of the battlefield, from the hurricane [promenade] deck, and during a heavy shower of rain. The bank hid the background from the sight; but from the slight view I got up through a ravine where a small branch made into the river, just below the batteries, I judged the ground to be quite considerably broken if not hilly.

I saw but little evidences or signs of the recent battle except the shattered and splintered stumps of trees standing near the water's edge and which had evidently been cut off by the enemy shots at our gunboats from their batteries. There appears to be a considerable camp of soldiers here, from the tents, and men *too*, which we see lining the banks. Our "calliope" is here called upon to display its musical skill as we pass them, as indeed it has been at any time heretofore when we were passing a point where troops were stationed.

Dover is here just above the fort or batteries, the most considerable town we have yet pass[ed] on the Tennessee [River]. It occupies a good site on the river, both as a commercial point, and a pleasant location. It has an old and now deserted appearance. It is the county seat of Stewart County, is on the south bank of the river, as is also the fort.

Just above the town is the Cumberland Ironworks, recently burned by the rebels, to keep them from falling into the hands of the government troops. The wreck, and site where they stood, is now almost submerged by water. It is said that John Bell, one of the recent candidates for President of the United States, was largely interested [invested] in these works.

BY THE DIM AND FLARING LAMPS:
THE CIVIL WAR DIARY OF SAMUEL MCILVAINE

The iron rolling mill was, in fact, owned by John Bell[13] of Tennessee, the Presidential candidate of the Constitutional Union Party. Bell finished fourth in the election of 1860, carrying Kentucky, Virginia, and Tennessee.[14] The Constitutional Union Party committed itself to preservation of the Union under the Constitution, but without taking a stand on slavery, and without defining whether the Constitution allowed the national government to use force to preserve the Union.[15]

Passing on from Fort Donaldson [Donelson], we soon meet with the Ohio & Mississippi Railroad, which running from Memphis strikes the river a short distance above Dover, and running around the bend of the river to Clarksburgh [Clarksville] crosses and pursues its way to Bowling Green, where it connects with the Great Southern Railway from Louisville, Kentucky. In many places this railroad runs under the high rocky bluffs of the river which have been blasted away to form the track, which in some places in the present high stage of the river is scarce above the water, and in one instance near the very small town of Palmyra, I observed a tunnel of about a quarter mile in length, through a high rocky bluff bank.

Passing on we arrive at Clarksville; here also the rebels have thrown up entrenchments to command the river. They [the entrenchments] are now in possession of our troops, a detachment of whom are stationed here. Clarksville is quite a considerable place, with many very fine buildings; both as storehouses and private residences and

---

13 Andrew H. Foote, "Report of Flag-Officer Andrew H. Foote, U. S. Navy", in *The War Of The Rebellion: A Compilation Of The Official Records of The Union And Confederate Armies*, Series 1, ed. Lt. Col. Robert N. Scott, (Washington: Government Printing Office, 1882), VII, 423.

14 Winthrop D. Jordan, Leon F. Litwack, et. al., *The United States Conquering A Continent*, 5th ed. (Englewood Cliffs, NJ: Prentice-Hall, 1982), p. 337.

15 Billings, p. 16.

public buildings. It is the county seat of Montgomery County, but no demonstrations of a Union feeling are at all perceivable as we pass the town, or rather, city. The railroad bridge here is only partially destroyed and might soon be restored.

Foote describes the rebel soldiers who escaped from Fort Donelson as "having wantonly burned the splendid railroad bridge near the city, against the remonstrances of the citizens."[16]

Passing on up a few miles we land, and take on a short string of fence (standing near the bank) for fuel. It being now near dark we tie up for the night. The *Lady Pike* soon comes alongside of us with the balance of our regiment. The banks and bluffs of the river continue to increase in height and rocky ruggedness as we proceed up.

Monday, March 3, 1862
Cumberland River

Start at daylight. The bluffs along the river increase in height and magnitude, rising in many places in perpendicular or overhanging cliffs to the height of 100 feet direct from the water's edge and alternating from one side to the other of the river, and then again retiring as it were from the channel of the river, leaving an extended low bottom, which is now entirely covered with water. The rain of yesterday and last night seem to keep the river up, and we pass many houses and farms completely flooded with the high water; and from which the inhabitants have fled. It would seem from appearances that the river is higher now than is common for it to get, even in time of high water.

The day is raw and cool and snow flying in the air. Gradually the heavy timber of the river bottom disappears, and the banks of the river

---

16 Foote, p. 423.

BY THE DIM AND FLARING LAMPS:
THE CIVIL WAR DIARY OF SAMUEL MCILVAINE

become covered with pretty groves of cedar of a natural growth. The country becomes more open, [and] pass more batteries with mounted cannon at a short turn in the river. These batteries are on a high bluff bank and arranged so as to completely command the river, although we have no account of their having been used at all against our boats in their ascent up the river to Nashville. Proceeding up, houses begin to dot the hills which here close in on either side near the river. [We] turn a bend in the river, see many steamers, houses thicken, and it becomes evident that we approach the city of Nashville, the hotbed of rebellion of this part of the country.

[We p]ass one of our ironclad gunboats lying on the opposite side of the river from the city while the banks of the river on the city side are lined with transport steamers. Pass up through the draw of the railroad bridge, which bridge is entirely destroyed (except the draw and piers), as well as the splendid suspension bridge which used to span the river here; and in which Zollicoffer is said to have had most of his worth in estate. Thus his family (comprising as I learn, a wife and several daughters) find themselves by this unholy rebellion stripped of all their property, as well as a husband and father. [These fine bridges were both destroyed by the rebels in the vain hope of staying the progress of the Union Army. This foolish business will be a serious detriment to the prosperity of the city, without retarding the movements of the Federal troops but slightly, as both troops and supplies can be brought up the river and landed in the city.] The Cumberland and Tennessee Rivers seem to have been formed purposely for carrying troops & supplies into the rebel territory to crush out this most monstrous rebellion, by their very course & termination, whilst that part of the army which has marched through via Bowling Green, can and are, being rapidly ferried across the river, several boats being engaged in this business. A long line of army wagons reaching along the road to the north as far as we can see, stand waiting their turn to cross.

Pass up toward the upper part of the city, and heave to alongside of another boat as we cannot find a place to land for boats. This was about eleven o'clock A.M. After a few moments, we drop down again and find a landing place below the bridge and proceed to unload and take our camp equipage, wagons, teams etc. ashore. Perceiving there would be plenty ... of leisure time, as quick as the boat was fairly landed and tied up, I jumped ashore, before the guard was posted, and proceeded to gratify my curiosity by taking a stroll through the city.

As the Statehouse occupies a commanding eminence, in fact the highest point in the city and not far distant, [I] make directly for that. As I pass along I observe quite an extensive scope and mostly covered with water, the streets being raised above the water by embankment; over a considerable portion of this low ground is built dwelling houses, the water rising to the second story in some of them. This is back water from the river, and will I presume mostly run off as soon as the river falls.

On reaching the Statehouse find it indeed a large and beautiful structure, built of a species of very fine freestone, abounding in this vicinity; I should judge from stepping the length and width, that it is fully 200 feet in length, by 120 in width. There is a splendid stone terrace running around the entire building, about twenty feet in width. This fine terrace is built up from the level of the ground with hewn stone, to the height of about eight or nine feet covered over perfectly level with large dressed stone.

There are four entrances to the building, one at either end, and one at either side. Opposite each of these entrances is a broad flight of stone steps, or stairs leading onto the top of the terrace while another short flight leads to the door; on either side of each pair of stairs stood a lamp post, and around each post were three life-sized statues, which I at first mistook for marble, but on a close inspection found to be cast. Two of the three were females representing the goddess of liberty. With one hand [each] held aloft over their head and shoulders, thin flowing drapery, which however fell very low in front exposing the naked bust. The two females faced toward [the] building. The other was a male representing an Indian warrior, holding aloft in one hand a flaming torch, whilst with the other, he grasped a quiver of arrows. He stood facing outward. There being three of these statues around each lamp post, the whole number around the building was 24.

BY THE DIM AND FLARING LAMPS:
THE CIVIL WAR DIARY OF SAMUEL MCILVAINE

I could not get into the house and therefore can say but little of the interior, however from an uncertain view through the window I could see that it was seated and furnished in very splendid style. And here I, "one of Lincoln's hirelings", stood alone, in this haughty city of rebellion, looking into the sumptuously furnished hall, where so recently sat an aristocratic and haughty assembly of traitors, planning and discussing measures of treason. Surely very strange things occasionally occur, and more especially in these times of war!

Leaving the Statehouse, I passed on a short distance, and was passing up a rather unfrequented street to the top of a rising ground to get a better view, when I was suddenly struck by the sight of this inscription:

> James Knox Polk
> 10th President of the U.S. Born
> November 2, 1795, Died June 15th, 1849

I was much surprised at this discovery, and could hardly believe the inscription, but assured myself of the fact, by enquiring of a young lady just then passing. Although I knew this was Polk's home, yet it had not entered my mind that I was so near the grave of one of the Presidents of the United States. The inscription which had arrested my attention was on the frieze of a dome of perhaps twelve feet in height, raised or resting on four stone columns over the vault, a large square slab or flag[stone] covered the vault, from which arose a square stone entablature to the height of about two feet, on which were other inscriptions, relating to his emigration to Tennessee in early life, and to other matters connected with his public career, etc.

The grave was in the yard, to a house which I judged had been the President's residence, a fact of which I afterward assured myself by enquiry, as well as the further fact of the residence there yet of his widow. Passing on, I turn into a street running more into the center of the city. I soon met with a man of whom I made some enquiry about Polk's family, and got into conversation with him. He soon professed Union sentiments, said there was a considerable Union element there but many were yet afraid to say anything in favor of the Union lest they should be marked by their secesh neighbors for future vengeance should they again get the ascendancy; said he had been living there for the last twelve years, had come from the North but had married here and had a family, and that all his interests were here. He believed the present Civil War was brought on by the leaders both of the abolition, as well as the Southern Rights parties. This was the only man with whom I essayed [attempted] a conversation.

Passing on into the heart of the city I see but little signs of life or business as a city. Almost every store is shut up. Passing one of the large buildings near the Public Square, I notice painted on it in large letters "Quartermaster's Office, C.S.A." Find the city to have considerable size or to cover a considerable area of ground, more than one would at first sight suppose, but it is very scatteringly built, but a small portion being compactly built together. It is very different from Louisville in this particular, although there are very many good, as well as very fine buildings.

C.S.A.: Confederate States of America.

During all my round[s] through the city, I saw but one Union flag. This appeared from the window of a private dwelling.

As I return to the boat, I stop a moment on the river bank at the foot of the column or pillar over which hung the wire cables of the suspension bridge. As I contemplate the ruin of the structure, I cannot but reflect on the folly and madness, which prompted [them] to such deeds. It is even said some of the military leaders would have burned the city could they have [effected] it.

It is cool and chilly this evening and the people here say it is the coldest spell of weather they have had here this winter. On returning to boat find our men undoing the wagons etc. in which I assist.

58

BY THE DIM AND FLARING LAMPS:
THE CIVIL WAR DIARY OF SAMUEL MCILVAINE

Tuesday, March 4, 1862
Nashville

Froze smartly last night; it however soon became very pleasant. This morn we go ashore and having handled some fires, get a breakfast once more by campfire, making coffee, broiling meat, etc. for ever since we have been on the boat we have a pretty hard chance to get anything to eat and a still worse one to get it cooked. Indeed, had not the engineers and boat's crew, ... been very clever and accommodating in allowing the men to occasionally broil a piece of meat at the furnace, and allowed us all the hot water we wanted from the boiler for our coffee, we would not have been able to cook anything at all... [F]or some reason which I could not learn, the quartermaster or his agent would scarce let us have rations enough to keep us from suffering with hunger, although there was plenty on board. So closely did he withhold it that the men took to stealing it to get enough to eat.

After getting breakfast and getting our camp equipage loaded, we are formed and marched through the city by [the] Statehouse, from the cupola of which floats the Stars and Stripes this morn, having been hoisted by some of the officers of our regiment. Passing the Statehouse, they turn a little aside to pass Polk's tomb, when opposite it the regiment is halted for a moment to look at it. I had, as had been my custom, stayed behind with the wagons, and on coming around by the tomb took occasion with three or four of my comrades to pass through the yard by the tomb. We enter through the gate of an iron fence which fronts the street (although an old and very ordinary board fence runs along one side the yard, and immediately by the tomb). A shell walk leads from the gate around the angle of the yard fence, and up a gentle ascent to the tomb and around it. Around the tomb are set out many very nice and pretty shrubs of various kinds, a few twigs of which I break off, and a single small shell from the walk as keepsakes.

As I stand by this last resting place of President Polk, I cannot avoid the reflection [that] however devoted, true and loyal a man he may have been to his country, and his whole country, yet he was selected by those in the interest of slavery, and slave extension, and elected to the important and responsible position of President of the United States by their efforts, for the express purpose of extending and strengthening that accursed institution; whether he was *wittingly* used for this purpose I leave others to judge.

The Mexican War was fought during President Polk's Administration. It was widely perceived then, as now, as a war started to give slavery room to expand; the Northwest Ordinance (1787) had prohibited slavery in the territories acquired from Britain in the Treaty of Paris, and the Missouri Compromise (1820) had prohibited slavery north of 36º 30' latitude in the Louisiana Purchase. The only option available for the expansion of slavery was to add more land to the United States.

We pass on through the yard to the back of the house where the well is. Here we draw some water (with a common windlass) and all take a drink. Although I was not in the [least] dry, I drink merely for the sake of drinking out of President Polk's well; as we passed through the yard there were no signs of a living individual perceivable about the house. Whether they were afraid of "Lincoln's hirelings", or whether they disdained to [show] themselves to our vulgar gaze, I know not, but presume the latter as I learn Mrs. Polk is avowedly and determinedly secesh in her proclivities.

The house is a moderate-sized, two story brick of but moderate pretensions, fronting to the streets on the east and north, on each of which streets is a short piece of iron fence, and in the east yard, a carriage way leads from the street gate, in a circle by the door and back to the gate. There was a veranda or portico supported by columns on the east and north or the two front sides of the house.

Passing out at the back gate near the well we go on, soon overtaking our regiment, which have gone out on the Charlottesville pike. As we pass out through the surburbs of the city, among the lower class of

BY THE DIM AND FLARING LAMPS:
THE CIVIL WAR DIARY OF SAMUEL MCILVAINE

the people, it is the only place in the city they deign to come out of their houses and show themselves to us.

While stopped a moment near some of these houses, got into conversation with some of the people. Among other enquiries they had was what regiment we were. Upon learning we were the 10th Indiana, a Negro standing by said that [the 10th Indiana] was one of the regiments in the Battle of Laurelhill, Virginia. Said he was there as a servant to Gen. Anderson, "And" said I, "you had to run did you?" He replied they did [run] like good fellows, and in running from Laurelhill they run almost into Rosecrans' hands before they knew it, and came very near being taken. I asked him where Gen. Anderson was now, he said he didn't know, "When you folks all come in heah, he left, and I dono whah he went to."

Union General William Starke Rosecrans (1819-1898): Rosecrans' early service was notable as an excellent strategist; his excessive caution, followed by a serious mistake at the Battle of Chickamauga (September 19-20, 1863), led Gen. Grant to remove him from command of the Army of the Cumberland.[17] After the war, he was Minister to Mexico, Congressman from California (1881-1885), and Register of the United States Treasury.[18]

We go out on Charlottesville pike about four miles and pitch our camp in a very beautiful grassy situation. Receive and put up our new tents this evening. They are the Sibley tent, circular at the base, about fifteen feet in diameter at base, and rise in shape of cone to the height of about fifteen feet. Five are allowed to each company. They are much handier and much more convenient than the old ones; in these we can stand upright without difficulty while in the old ones we could

---

[17] "Rosecrans, William Starke", *Encyclopedia Brittanica*, 1983, Micropaedia VIII, pp. 672-673.

[18] "Rosecrans, William Starke", *Encyclopedia Americana*, 1963, XXIII, 696.

only maintain an upright position immediately under the ridge pole. These are also arranged for building [a] fire in them.

The Sibley tent was named for Henry Sibley, who either invented it, or who commanded soldiers who did. The appearance and design are quite similar to an Indian tepee, with provisions for a wood stove to be used inside. Because of its size and expense, the Sibley tent fell out of field use in 1862.[19]

During the evening, two or three batteries of artillery come in and camp near us, whilst the tents of many other regiments begin to whiten the landscape in nearly every direction. As we pass out to our camping ground, we pass many splendid farms and residences fitted up with great taste. Much wealth and aristocracy is apparent on every hand. Not one of these splendid houses deigns to open their doors, or their inmates (if I except the Negroes), show themselves as we pass by.

After camping I sauntered off as I frequently do to look around a little, pass near where a couple of slaves are chopping wood. One of them a [mere] boy, the other quite an intelligent man, from whom I learn many interesting particulars, in regard to the evacuation of Nashville by the rebels, and the entrance of our troops. From his unvarnished, but (as I have not the least doubt) entirely truthful account, it would seem that the people were wellnigh frightened out of their wits, when it was learned by them that the Yankees were coming. Assemblies at church on Sunday, when it was learned and announced by the preacher that the Union soldiers were coming, and would be in the city in an hour & half, broke up in the wildest confusion. Scattering homeward, [they] began packing up some of the most valuable or necessary articles, with which ... with their families, [were] gathered into such vehicles as [were] most accessible, and fled like

---

19 Billings, pp. 46-48.

BY THE DIM AND FLARING LAMPS:
THE CIVIL WAR DIARY OF SAMUEL MCILVAINE

frightened sheep, while some of the numerous *generals* & *colonels*, so abundant in the South proposed to fight the Yankees to the death.

Samuel, like many other Northerners, found the Southern fascination with military titles (both real and honorary) most amusing.

Other leaders proposed to burn the city, but there was little time now to act on [the proposal]; the dreaded gunboats would be there soon. Something must be done speedily. Failing to arouse the chivalrous citizens to a determination to defend their homes, the batteries below the city, planted to dispute the passage of the river, were dismantled; most of the guns spiked, the magazine blown up. Teams were [im]pressed and such of the commissary stores as they had time to move were speedily moved to various places and secreted. Much meat was drawn to and thrown into the river. A considerable quantity of cotton pledged to the Confederate Government or used as breastworks at the batteries was taken possession of [and] attempted to be secreted by different individuals as their own property. Notwithstanding all their exertions large amounts of commissary stores fell into the hands of our troops.

"Spiking a gun" rendered a muzzleloading cannon temporarily unusable by driving a plug into the vent hole.

Samuel's account suggests that goods owned by the Confederate Government were being taken by individuals for the good of the Confederacy. In fact, the Confederate Army made repeated efforts to prevent bacon and other

Confederate-owned goods from being stolen by the population during the chaos just before the Union Army arrived.[20]

Perhaps the fright they received may account in part for their refusal to open their doors or to be seen by us as we pass, although it is now a week since our first troops entered the city. They told the slaves horrible tales of terrible treatment they were to receive at the hands of the Yankees to induce them to run off South with them. Many of them [the slaves] were seized promiscuously by the military leaders, rushed off with them South, [although] some of them succeeded in effecting their escape and returned to their old homes again.

This Negro seemed to think the war was somehow to result in favor of the slaves, or some way to their advantage, despite the tales their masters told them of the horrible treatment they were to receive from the Yankees. He also said he thought he ought to be free, and felt fully able to provide for and take care of himself.

Wednesday March 5, 1862

Pretty cool last night, and continues cool through the day. Receive new camp kettles and mess pans today and some clothing, especially pants. The word was that we must all have pants alike, of the sky blue color, consequently I drew another pair although I had one good pair already.

The Quartermaster also issued ten days' rations. There was considerable grumbling over this, as it was not in accordance with army regulations, and it was argued that it would [be] used too lavishly or wasted and the men would be out of rations before the ten days were up. The Quartermaster excused himself by saying he was satisfied we should remain here for that length of time & therefore he offered the

---

20 John B. Floyd, "Report of Brig. Gen. John B. Floyd, C. S. Army," in *The War Of The Rebellion: A Compilation Of The Official Records of The Union And Confederate Armies*, Series 1, ed. Lt. Col. Robert N. Scott, (Washington: Government Printing Office, 1882), VII, 428-429.

ten days' rations and they could take them or let it alone. Notwithstanding the grumbling, I believe the ten days' rations were taken by all the companies, each company setting up a commissary of its own to take care to preserve the rations.

We also changed our encampment a few rods across a little branch [stream] and pitch it on a hillside in a fine old woods pasture. The other regiments of our brigade (*viz.*) the 4th and 10th Kentucky and the 14th Ohio pitch their tents near us during the day. Several more batteries of artillery arrive and take up their position where we first camped, and the whole country seems dotted over with tents, in every direction as far as we can see, and there is a continual rumbling kept up by the [constant] passage of army wagons over the pike.

A rod is 16.5 feet.

I make a short excursion this evening to a neighboring hilltop nearby. Am much delighted with the beauty of the scenery, and richness of the soil.

Thursday, March 6, 1862

Snow on the ground this morning, and snowing when we get up; continues cold and blustering, with snow flying. There being plenty of good ash and hickory wood right in our camp, we pitch into it with a hearty good will, and soon have good fires to cook by and stand or sit around. Our mess [has] succeeded in fetching our little sheet iron stove, [which] we got at Lebanon, Kentucky, and [we] find it quite convenient [to] make a fire in our tent.

Nothing of importance occurs in camp except a rumored evacuation of Columbus, Kentucky, by the rebels, and the taking of two of the men of [our] company who have been sick several days, W. Sheetz and J. Coffman, to the hospital in the city.

THE DIARY
MARCH ENTRIES

The Confederate garrison at Columbus completed its evacuation on March 2nd.[21]

Friday, March 7, 1862

Sun rises clear, continues clear all day, gets quite pleasant. Snow is soon all lost in the bright sunshine. The surgeon has all the clothing put out to air.

Lt. Miller of Company F dies today in camp of congestion of the bowels. He has been very sick for the last two or three days, but now will be seen no more in our midst. He was a very fine clever fellow full of life and fun, and a good officer and will be much missed by the boys of his own company at least. His remains were sent home to his friends. William Stephens of Company H, a private, also dies today. I believe he was buried near the city, but am not certain.

The evacuation of Columbus is confirmed today. Thus is the rebel army completely cleared from Kentucky whilst we also have the proud capital of Tennessee ... in our possession. There is also a rumor afloat of the taking of Memphis by our troops. I was on guard today, it being the first detail since we came here.

The rumor was incorrect. Memphis was not taken by Union troops until June 6th.[22]

Saturday, March 8, 1862

Frosty and cool last night, but the sun rises clear, soon melting all the frost, and dispelling the cool air. The day becomes very fine.

---

21 E. B. Long, *The Civil War Day By Day*, (Garden City, NY: Doubleday & Co., 1971), p. 177.
22 Long, pp. 222-223.

BY THE DIM AND FLARING LAMPS:
THE CIVIL WAR DIARY OF SAMUEL MCILVAINE

I was called on this morning by Capt. Taylor to assist him, and Lt. [Job H.] Van Natta, in making out or rather transferring descriptive roll to the books. It must be done very accurately and requires very careful persons to do it properly. The rumor still continues of the taking of Memphis with a large amount of prisoners.

We have the first dress parade this eve ... since we came here, and the first since leaving Mill Spring in Kentucky. The regiment [is] commanded during the exercise by Major Miller, as both Col. Manson and Col. Kise are under arrest. We learn that the adjutant [to Col.] Kise is also added to the number under arrest from our regiment. It is said (how true I know not) [they are under arrest] for cursing Gen. Thomas, whilst we *now* learn that Col. Kise was arrested for making a false report of the part his regiment took in the Battle of Mill Spring. Yet all who have witnessed their action in that engagement almost to a man acknowledge the truthfulness of the report.

Three of our sick men left at Mill Spring come into camp this eve, (*viz.*) Swisher, Ross, and Shambaugh, and are warmly greeted.

Sunday, March 9, 1862

Moderate today but cloudy and indicative of rain, but little of importance going on in camp. I assist Lt. Van Natta in making out the payroll part of the day, write a letter or partially write one to my Aunt D. Rhodes also today.

Monday, March 10, 1862

Rained pretty hard last night, and still rains some this morn; but finally clears off and becomes pleasant.

Nothing of particular importance going on in camp today. I learn, however, that Col. Manson's trial comes on today, and further that he has instituted a suit of enquiry, or an investigation of the allegations against him, when if they [are] found to be unjust or untrue the case will, of course, be dismissed.

I continue to assist Lt. Van Natta with the payrolls.

A rumor prevails in camp today that some of our wagons and men (*i.e.*, the wagons belonging to the army camped near the city) were taken by a gang of Texan Rangers, but were pursued and retaken again. It is also said their colonel was taken in the city, having dress[ed] in [civilian] clothing and slipped in to make observations.

Finish my letter to my Aunt Dianah Rhodes and mail it.

Tuesday, March 11, 1862

Assist Lt. [Van Natta] at the payrolls.

Cool in the night, but gets very pleasant today.

Nothing of importance going on in camp. We had a visit today from Chaplain Stephenson of the 15th Indiana, which regiment have just come in via Bowling Green and crossed the river. The meeting between Mr. Stephenson, his son, & Capt. Taylor, was warm and cordial, much good-natured sparring was done about not writing more promptly, etc. Then each had a tale to tell [of] events and circumstances, which had happened [to] them since the last meeting, and quite a friendly quarrel raged for some time between them in respect to the bravery and prowess of their respective regiments.

Wednesday March 12, 1862

I am still engaged in assisting the lieutenant on the payrolls.

Extremely pleasant today.

Reporting in camp today that six men of the 9th Indiana on picket were killed last night. Nothing of importance in camp, except reading some orders on dress parade in regard to police regulations, report condition of arms, etc. Mailed a letter this morn to [my] brother William.

BY THE DIM AND FLARING LAMPS:
THE CIVIL WAR DIARY OF SAMUEL MCILVAINE

Thursday, March 13, 1862

Rained heavily in the night, with thunder & lightning, damp and [rainy] this morning, but clears off and becomes very pleasant toward evening. (I am still assisting the lieutenant on the payrolls today.)

Nothing of special importance occurs in camp today, except the reading on dress parade of the compliments and thanks of the President and Secretary of War to the brave soldiers who fought and conquered at Mill Spring. It was a proud moment for us when we received the thanks and praises of our President, for services we had rendered our government when the hour of danger and trial came.

Friday, March 14, 1862

Gloomy and rainy inclined this morn but clears off and is very pleasant in forenoon. [It] rains heavily in the evening, and continues to rain all night.

I go in company with Lt. Van Natta and G. W. Bannon to the bank of the river below the city to view the rebel fortifications and guns which they so speedily ran away from at the approach of our gunboats, without even firing one of theirs (except to set fire to the gun carriages, part of which were burned). [We] found several (I think about a dozen) mostly heavy guns, some of them were U.S. pieces, others had been cast by the rebels and bore the manufacturer's mark at Richmond, Virginia. Some of the guns were dismounted, the carriages partially burned and most of them spiked.

"U.S. pieces" refers to cannon seized by Confederate forces from U.S. arsenals at the beginning of the war.

They had a magazine here, formed by digging a pit in the side of the hill and covering [it] with railroad iron and earth. This they had blown up, being unable to get it removed, so speedy was the descent of our troops upon them. The iron railings [were] blown in every direction, some of them mowing off the tops of trees in their aerial flight and landing some twenty rods from the point whence they were projected. Other[s] had been elevated into the air and falling end foremost had run into the earth fully one third their length, which was sixteen or eighteen feet). Others were twisted and bent, until they looked like huge black snakes writhing and twisting in the sunshine. A perfect shower of ball and shell covered the ground for a distance around, in size from a canister up to a sixty-four pounder. Some were round, others conical.

"Canister", or canister shot, was an artillery projectile rather like a shotgun shell, but much larger. It consisted of a small number of iron balls exceeding one inch diameter each, sandwiched in between two iron plates, packed with sawdust to prevent movement of the shot during handling, and wrapped in tin packaging. Canister shot was fired at soldiers at ranges of 300 to 600 yards, with devastating effect.[23]

After looking around to our satisfaction, we return to camp passing on our return through a beautiful grove of cedars occupying a knoll of oblong shape. This grove had evidently been at some former time fitted up as a pleasure ground [park]; an old carriage drive was plainly distinguishable running around near the border, but it now has the appearance of having been used as a feed ground for stock.

Pluck some little flowers, the first of the season, which I will send in letters to my friends. Get news today of Union victory in Arkansas; also the news that the rebels had fallen back from Manassas Junction [Virginia].

---

[23] Warren Ripley, *Artillery and Ammunition of the Civil War*, (New York: Van Nostrand Reinhold Co., 1970), p. 267-268.

BY THE DIM AND FLARING LAMPS:
THE CIVIL WAR DIARY OF SAMUEL MCILVAINE

Saturday, March 15, 1862

Rains all day with very little intermission, but quite slowly and moderately.

I learn that Col. Manson's investigation is still progressing. Nothing of importance in camp, except that our regiment is called on to furnish one hundred men to go on picket duty this evening. Spend the day in writing, reading, etc.

Sunday, March 16, 1862

Rather cool and cloudy today. The matter of interest in camp today is the appearance of the Paymaster with Uncle Sam's strongbox. The regiments are paid off today, this being the second payment since we have been in the service, and notwithstanding [that] four months' pay are now due us, we receive pay only for two, or pay up to last of December.

There are some rumors of moving us from here tomorrow.

Our pickets bring in a deserter from the rebel army this evening. He tells us that the rebel army did not tarry long at Murfreesburrow, but continued their flight to Alabama, and that in the brush near the borders of that State, he made his escape from them. Says he was formerly from Illinois and being in Tennessee at the breaking out of war was forced into the rebel service. I am on guard today.

Rutherford County, of which Murfreesboro is the county seat, is the county adjoining Nashville to the southeast. Apparently the rebel army retreated in this direction as they left Nashville.

THE DIARY
MARCH ENTRIES

Monday, March 17, 1862

Cool this morning. Nothing of particular importance occurs in camp today. I [received] two or three shirts, pair [of] drawers, etc. today. Write letter to my cousin Mary McIlvaine this evening.

Tuesday, March 18, 1862

Cool this morning, but gets very pleasant in evening.
Nothing of particular importance going on immediately in camp. Learn the adjutant's trial is now before the court, and that on an investigation Col. Manson's persecutors were glad to drop the case, without going into a trial in his case.

Persecutors? Prosecutors? In light of how he felt about Col. Manson and the charges against him, Samuel could have meant either word.

Learn that after all our trouble and time spent in making out the payrolls, they are wrong and will not answer. They gave us the wrong kind of forms; ... therefore they will have to be made over again. Consequently, ... Capt. Taylor calls on me again today to assist Lt. Van Natta in making out the new rolls, and in the meantime, he goes into the city to get his resignation and discharge papers signed by Gen. Buell.
The report is this evening that we are to march tomorrow morning; the sick are sent into the hospital in [the] city, and other preparations made. Five or six sick men from our company are sent in.
As we expect to go south and have already sufficient loads to carry without our overcoats and expect to have little use for them soon, many are boxing up their coats and sending them home. I also put in an augur and an ax, which I got at Mill Spring, and have brought thus far with me, together with a rebel knapsack, get and box [them] into one of

BY THE DIM AND FLARING LAMPS:
THE CIVIL WAR DIARY OF SAMUEL MCILVAINE

the wagons going in with the sick. We don't get into the city until after dark, and have considerable difficulty in finding the Express office, and after finding it further difficulty awaits us (for I had gone with others on the same business) in getting our business transacted, as they are about closing up for the night. I wished to pay the expressage on our box and take a receipt but they refused to give any receipt, or to insure their safe delivery, in consequence of the dangers on the route. I therefore declined to pay the expressage, preferring to leave it to our friends at home to pay, should they succeed in going through safe. I therefore leave them at the office and make my way back to camp. [I] was lucky enough to find a wagon going out in which I got an opportunity to ride back.

Wednesday, March 19, 1862

Rained heavily last night, and continues for a while this morn, but finally clears off and becomes pleasant. There is some excitement in our company today in regard to filling the vacant offices created by the resignation of the captain and two lieutenants; it is expected and desired by the whole company that the 1st Lt. J. Van Natta will become our captain. But [it] is learned by the men that a certain Ludlow (who has been acting as sergeant major) is seeking office of 1st Lieutenant in our company. He is not liked by any of the men, who think we have men in our own company fully as competent for the office as he is, and on his speaking to Lt. Van Natta in regard to the matter, and claiming it as his right by regular promotion, he [Lt. Van Natta] gave him to understand that if the company wanted him and would *elect* him, that it would all be right. He further expressed his intention that so far as he had anything to do with it, or any influence in the matter, the company should have the privilege of filling the vacancies by an election from among themselves.

Write to Barns & McConnell at Oxford, Indiana, in regard [to] our box of overcoats. I also write to my wife's sister Sarah Brown, and her daughter, in answer to letters recently received from them.

THE DIARY
MARCH ENTRIES

Thursday, March 20, 1862

The camp is early alive this morn, with preparations to march. The day very fine with a breeze from the southwest. The whole division strike[s] tents and starts, taking the road to the city. We pass through the southwestern portion by the penitentiary. A rather small yard is here walled in, with a very strong and high stone wall. We here part with, and take leave of Capt. Taylor and Lt. Sappington, or rather they take leave of the company and start home this morning. I send home to my family with Capt. Taylor $.50 having borrowed $.30 of it of [from] a couple of [the] members of our company ... ($.20 of S. Horner, and $.10 of W.J. Page) for that purpose until our next payment. Col. Manson goes home on furlough.

Probably $30, $20, and $10 are the actual amounts; he refers in his letter of September 29th to a very similar arrangement, but definitely for tens of dollars, not tens of cents.

The people appear much more willing to see us than when we first passed through the city. The women of this city have been particularly careful to manifest their hatred and ill will to the Union troops on all occasions when they could get an opportunity. Indeed so sure an indication of the general feelings of the population in regard to the great difficulty which is now arraying one portion of the people against the other, father against son, and brother against brother, is found in the expressions of the fair sex on the subject; that they, as a general thing may be taken as a pretty sure indication of that feeling.

For instance, if the general feeling of the population of a city or district of country is for the Union, it is sure to manifest itself when Union troops are passing through, in some way through the medium of the fair sex, either by waving of handkerchiefs and flags, and shouts for the Union; or in the more substantial way of sundry kind acts toward the soldiers, in the gift of pies, cakes, milk, and other luxuries, which

BY THE DIM AND FLARING LAMPS:
THE CIVIL WAR DIARY OF SAMUEL MCILVAINE

the soldier seldom gets. On the other hand, if the general feelings of the population are with the traitors, however guarded the expressions of the men are in the presence of Union troops, the general feeling of the people are sure to find vent in sundry expressions of contempt, ill will, and general antipathy of the women. I have heard several anecdotes illustrative of this fact since we have been here, two or three of which I will give.

As the 15th Indiana were marching through the city, with colors flying, and playing the national air "Hail, Columbia", a lady (pardon the expression, I mean only a woman) standing at her door called out, "You had better play Bull's Run, double quick."

Soon after Gen. Buell occupied the city, as he was passing a large and very fine residence, the woman of the house, being at the door, chose to give vent to some insulting and contemptuous expression in his hearing, in regard to the Union troops. He turned square around and taking a look at her house said, "I think, Madam, your house would make an excellent hospital," and rode on. In half an hour after, this woman had the gratification to see her fine house taken possession of by a guard of Union soldiers, and loads of sick men arrive at her door.

A week or two after the city was entered by our troops, as a regiment from one of the Northern states was passing through, a woman standing at her yard gate, observing the long lines of troops that continued to pass through the city, enquired of a soldier, "How far does your army reach back yet?" "By G-d, Madam, it reaches to the North Pole, and when I left there was another regiment or two trying to get in," was the rough, but rather significant reply.

Surprising as it may seem to a modern audience, there was a time when the Biblical injunction against "taking the name of the Lord in vain" was taken seriously, and even a quotation would edit profane language.

THE DIARY
MARCH ENTRIES

Our regiment pass on until we arrive at the house where Parson Brownlow is stopping, he having just entered the city a day or two since from the rebel prison at Knoxville. Here the regiment were halted a moment and faced about to greet this veteran hero and Unionist. He came out and said, "Go on boys, I am with you; give grape to the masses and hemp to the leaders." The regiment gave him three rousing cheers and passed on. He looked much emaciated and worn down with his recent imprisonment.

William Gannaway Brownlow (1805-1877): A Methodist minister, political agitator, and journalist. While not opposed to slavery, he strongly opposed secession, and was imprisoned by the Confederates as a traitor. He was released to the Union March 3rd. After the war, he served two terms as governor of Tennessee, where he opposed black suffrage, and proposed removing them to a separate territory. In 1869, he was elected to the U.S. Senate.[24]

"Grape", of course refers to grapeshot, and "hemp" refers to rope. Rest assured that Parson Brownlow was not suggesting a wine and marijuana party for the Confederates.

Leaving the city, we go out south on the Franklin pike. As we pass out of the city, I observe peach trees in bloom, and as we continue our march, they become more frequent and the road is lined with their beautiful bloom, fair and beautiful as the first blushes of the maiden.

We march about nine miles from the city through a most pleasant and beautiful country in a high state of cultivation, fine and tasteful houses, with beautifully laid out and ornamented yards and gardens. Pass [many] stone walls around farms.

---

[24] "Brownlow, William Gannaway", *Encyclopedia Americana*, 1963, IV, 621-622.

BY THE DIM AND FLARING LAMPS:
THE CIVIL WAR DIARY OF SAMUEL MCILVAINE

Friday, March 21, 1862

Quite cool today, with even a little snow flying.

Strike tents early and wait a long time for passing troops before we can get the road, but when we finally get started, travel steadily until dark. When we camp, the men are all very tired and weary.

We passed through Franklin, the county seat of Williamson County [Tennessee] today. It is a smart little town with a good courthouse, and is surrounded with a good country. We pass a good many cotton fields, with the old stalks still standing, as well as several cotton presses and ginning houses before we get to Franklin. Before reaching Franklin, pass a smart range of hills where the country is much broken and rocky. The country for some distance south of Franklin is very good, when it becomes more broken again.

We pass a large encampment of troops this evening with several field batteries which I learn is McCook's Division. On our march today, we passed several fields where Negro women were plowing in the fields with the men, in others they were cutting the old corn stalks, and pulling the old cotton stalks or weeds and piling them to burn.

Almost certainly, "McCook's Division" is Brig. Gen. Alexander McCook's Second Division of the Army of the Ohio. There is necessarily some uncertainty in this, however, since a total of 17 McCook family members fought on the Union side, many of them reaching the rank of general.[25,26]

Saturday, March 22, 1862

Quite cool today, with a little snow and rain falling at intervals.

---

[25] Boatner, p. 526.
[26] Boatner, pp. 528-529.

THE DIARY
MARCH ENTRIES

As McCook's Division is passing today, we do not move. I assist some at the payrolls again today. As we were encamped near a cotton plantation with a gin and ginning house, I take the opportunity to visit and examine them. Notwithstanding I have seen many accounts and frequently read of the famous "Cotton Gin", yet not until I [had] seen one did I have any definite or correct idea of its appearance or mode of operation.

The building in which the ginning is done is usually a large barn-like structure, one part of which is raised on large wooden posts forming an open shed. In this is a large wooden cog wheel turned by horse or mule power. Into the large wheel smaller ones are geared with bands to connect with and run the gin, which is placed in a large room upstairs. Into this room, the cotton as picked from the fields is carried by the slaves in large baskets and emptied, preparatory to being ginned or separated from the seed.

The gin is a very simple contrivance, and consists of a small cylinder or rather a shaft, upon which are arranged at intervals of some two inches, small circular steel plates, something like a very small circular saw. Around the outer circle or edge of these plates is formed a set of very fine teeth similar to sickle teeth. This cylinder or shaft, with its series of circular saws, revolves in a concave not unlike that of a common threshing machine, but in the lower or under edge of the concave, is a small slit [cut] as if sawed in the steel plate with a hand saw. There is one of these slits in the concave for every one of the revolving plates on the cylinder, and just wide enough to let them pass through edgewise. A quantity of cotton is placed in the machine, on and around the cylinder. The lid [is] shut down and the gin started. The sharp sickle teeth catch the cotton, jerking it through the slits in the concave, which are not wide enough to let the seed pass through. On the underside a series of little brushes are arranged, which brush the cotton out of the teeth, and a fan blows it, light and loose as down, through a chute into a tight room from which it is taken and baled up. I noticed that there was invariably attached to each cotton house & gin, [a] pair of stones for cracking corn, for the slaves of the plantation.

BY THE DIM AND FLARING LAMPS:
THE CIVIL WAR DIARY OF SAMUEL MCILVAINE

There was quite a considerable excitement raised this evening in our bunk, by the discovery that the "Zollicoffer" or "Southern body guards", had made their debut among us, and had snugly secreted and stowed themselves away in our clothing, ready to pounce upon their unwary victims when asleep. Shirts were jerked off, hurriedly examined, and many of them committed to the flames.

A variety of lice bedeviled soldiers throughout the war, due both to a lack of bathing, as well as a shortage of proper laundry facilities.

Sunday, March 23, 1862

Cool this morning. Strike tents pretty early. Whilst packing up, and loading our camp equipage, the Negroes, both male and female, flock into the camp in great numbers to gather the cast off clothing. They frequently get a considerable amount of clothing, particularly when there has been an encampment for several days or a week or two; I have frequently seen good army overcoats thrown away, or sold for a pie or two or a few cakes, or a little bread merely because the owner was tired of carrying them.

We pass through Springhill [Maury County, Tennessee]. Turning west here, we go out about a mile, and camp in open pasture ground near the railroad track. A large number of tents are pitched around this little town.

I indulge this evening in a game of ball with the boys. It is the first ball playing I have engaged in a long time. The day has been quite cool and raw, with a smart spilling of snow several times through the day.

Monday, March 24, 1862

Pretty cool this morning.

Take a walk over a part of the Widow Brown's extensive plantation, whose house is near our camp, and in one of whose outhouses, it is said a large amount of bacon was found (represented to be a houseful). (It [had] been run out here by the rebels from Nashville on the railroad [and] stowed away). The place seems mainly devoted to raising grain and stock. I saw several stockyards of grain, hay, etc., houses and cribs of corn. During all my walk, the snow fell in downy flakes, but melted as fast as it struck the ground.

Lt. Van Natta is quite sick today. [He] made an attempt to work at payrolls this morn, but he was too sick ... to [work and] quit it. I, however, continued to work at them, writing the names, etc.

Capt. [James H.] Boyl returns today, having left us while at Mill Spring. He brings some recruits with him. Represents produce and stock to be very low in our part of the country, yet that business was going ahead there uninterruptedly.

It has been rather cool all day.

Tuesday, March 25, 1862

Sun shines out clear and beautiful, is a delightful day.

I continue to write on the payrolls. Lt. Van Natta still too unwell to help at them. Nothing of any special importance in camp.

Wednesday, March 26, 1862

Weather very fine today, a breeze balmy and pleasant.

Work at payrolls again today. The lieutenant [is] still too unwell to assist. The regiment have a short drill this evening.

The subject of electing company officers comes up again this evening. It had been said that Col. Manson declared before he left, that the offices must be filled by regular promotion. We had also heard today through a letter to Lt. Van Natta from home that our orderly sergeant had died at Sommerset. To fill the offices by regular

BY THE DIM AND FLARING LAMPS:
THE CIVIL WAR DIARY OF SAMUEL MCILVAINE

[promotion] would put into the office of first lieutenant our second sergeant, a man who had had several difficulties with members of the company, and [is] generally disliked. He was also addicted to drink somewhat, although when on good terms with one he was very clever and accommodating, but was rather high tempered & rather easily fretted, and it was generally thought by the men [that] he ought not to have the office and hoped he would not get it, and were confident he would not, if it were left to a vote to fill the vacancies. Yet he claimed it, and insisted that it was his right; it was thought and believed by many that he had got on the fair side of Col. Manson, and that he would have him commissioned whilst he [Col. Manson] was gone to Indiana. Notwithstanding all this, the impression seemed to prevail that we could have an election if [we were] right energetic about it. Therefore a good deal of talk and argument was had, but amounted to nothing. It is rumored also in addition to the death of our orderly, that several others of our company had died also at Sommerset.

There was quite an excitement sprung up in camp between the 9th Ohio Volunteers and the 18th Regulars, camped side [by] side, and near us. It was caused by some of the officers of the Regulars tying up a man by the thumbs to the limb of a tree so high that his toes just touched the ground, for some trifling offense. One version of it was that he was tied up by the toes with his head down, but as I did not see him, and there were so many rumors about it, I give the mildest [version] (preferring not to exaggerate a thing already too bad), but be the facts as they may as [to] which end was down, the sturdy Dutchmen of the Ohio 9th looked on until they could brook it no longer, and [a] party went over and cut him down, or attempted it. In this humane act they were resisted by the officers of the Regulars, and a general melee ensued in which some of the officers got knocked over with [clubs] of wood, and the excitement ran so high for a few moments, that it threatened to be serious. I was told the Dutchmen threatened to go over *en masse* and clean them out, but the difficulty was finally quieted without much bloodshed. It was asserted that the man who was hung up died by reason of it, but I was not able to learn this was certain.

THE DIARY
MARCH ENTRIES

Accounts by other Civil War soldiers suggest that "tying a man up by thumbs" was not an uncommon punishment.[27]

Volunteer regiments had responded to President Lincoln's call for soldiers to serve three years or the duration of the war; Regulars were regiments of the peacetime army. Note that Volunteer regiments were numbered by State, while the Regulars were not. Secretary of the Treasury Salmon P. Chase, responsible for organizing the volunteer regiments, described the popular sentiment in terms of his native State by saying that he would "rather have no regiments raised in Ohio than that they should not be known as Ohio regiments."[28]

The "sturdy Dutchmen" were actually Germans. The Ohio 9th Infantry Regiment, sometimes known as "German Turners", consisted largely of German refugees from the unsuccessful 1848 Revolution. Samuel's confusion was doubtless caused by the similarity between "Dutch" and the German word for "German", *Deutsch*. (A similar confusion in Pennsylvania gives us the misnomer "Pennsylvania Dutch".)

Thursday, March 27, 1862

A very fine day, the breeze blows with a balmy and exhilarating effect.

Nothing of special importance in camp today. Assist Lt. Van Natta (who is better today) to finish the payrolls, this being the second set we

---
[27] Billings, p. 156.
[28] Nevins, pp. 168-169.

BY THE DIM AND FLARING LAMPS:
THE CIVIL WAR DIARY OF SAMUEL MCILVAINE

have made out for the same payment. The boys engage in ball playing, in which I take a part this evening. We get ... mail this evening with late papers, the news still of a glorious character for us.

Friday, March 28, 1862

An exceedingly pleasant [day], but with a light shower in the evening.

Write some in journal today (which has gotten behind, whilst employed on payrolls), engage in game [of] ball with the boys this evening. Detailed on guard this evening. Have a drill this afternoon in a field near by and in which several Negro women and men are engaged in plowing. They are breaking up a very rough piece of soddy, stumpy ground. The rumor very current in camp this evening [is] that the man, whom it is said the officers of the Regulars hung by the heels yesterday, had died.

Saturday, March 29, 1862

Indications of rain this morning. Alternate sunshine and clouds today.

Preparations going on to resume our march this morning. I go on guard after breakfast. Strike our tents, load up, and start about ten o'clock.

Pass through a very fine country with an exceedingly rich soil, and to all appearances large plantations, with large and stately mansions or dwellings; cotton fields are frequent, in some the old stalks still standing, in others the slaves pulling them up, piling them & burning them. Cotton houses with ginning apparatus & press, and the never-failing corn cracker, are quite common. Ploughing is going on in which many slave women are engaged along with the men. Pass field of oats already up.

Cross a small stream on a temporary foot bridge, built (I learn) by one of our Indiana regiments. The country on either side of this creek for some distance [is] quite broken. Camp quite late in a thick woods of heavy timber, a short distance north of Columbia [seat of Maury County, Tennessee]. The timber around our camp has not been cut ... much and is of an excellent quality.

Sunday, March 30, 1862

Very fine today. The sun comes down quite hot.

We do not march today. I take a short walk this morning through the old woods & over the hills adjacent to the camp. The peach trees on the surrounding plantations (of which there [are] large amounts), now in full bloom, present a rich and exceedingly pleasant appearance; the redbud also begins to put forth its bloom. The timber is of large poplar, ash, sugartree, oak, hickory etc. and is of a fine quality. I spend the day in writing, reading, etc.

Another unfortunate accident happened in our camp today. One of the men in Company K of our regiment accidentally shot himself through the breast with his pistol, which fell out of his belt or pocket while stooping for something, and striking on the rock with muzzle up, went off. It did not kill him immediately, but he will hardly live.

Our sick are examined this evening and all who are unable to march are sent to the hospital & barracks at Columbia, with their descriptive lists and five days' rations. Among those from our company [were] A. Campbell, J.W. Coffman & others.

BY THE DIM AND FLARING LAMPS:
THE CIVIL WAR DIARY OF SAMUEL MCILVAINE

Monday, March 31, 1862

Indicated rain last night, but none fell. It is, however, considerably cooler today. We did not march today, and I assisted in getting the clothing accounts with the men on the books. Nothing of importance in camp.

April Entries

Tuesday, April 1, 1862

A very pleasant day, the air balmy and fragrant with the early spring blossoms; we still remain camped today, but little of importance occurs in camp today. Read & write etc.

I go over into the camp of the 18th Regulars this evening, the guard telling me as I passed in, that any of the soldiers from the neighboring camps were admitted, except those of the 9th Ohio. Witness their guard mounting, find it very tedious and ceremonious, contrasted with our own simple (and I think fully as effective) guard mounting, done according to the same army regulations, but in less than half the time.

A rumor of the taking of Island No. 10 creates quite a commotion and excitement among the boys in camp today. Many of our boys ... visit the Indiana 15th & 40th Regiments, which are passing the road today, for our camp is off the road a short distance.

The rumor was incorrect; Island Number Ten was taken April 8th.[29]

Wednesday April 2, 1862

Quite warm today.

Strike tents about ten o'clock, and start on our march south. The poplar leaves are beginning to spread. Pass over Duck River, on a temporary bridge put [up] for the crossing of the army, and which we have been waiting for, the rebels in their flight having destroyed the bridge over this stream. This stream is hardly large enough to be

---

29 Mitchell, John B., "Island Number 10", *Encyclopedia Americana*, 1984, XV, 510.

BY THE DIM AND FLARING LAMPS:
THE CIVIL WAR DIARY OF SAMUEL MCILVAINE

called a river, yet when high runs a great deal of water. There is also a pontoon bridge here.

Columbia [is] the county seat of Maury County, and quite a considerable town, with some good buildings ([except] the old-fashioned square courthouse, and quite old looking) and a large and fine building in which is ... a school called the "Hoiden School".

Camp 1 1/2 miles south [of] Columbia. Made but little progress today [on] account of having to wait on those ahead so much. The country through here is quite broken, but very pleasant. Have felt quite unwell today, & dull and drowsy yesterday.

Thursday, April 3, 1862

Very warm and dusty marching today. Started early and travel till late in the evening. Duck River crossed and the divisions ahead of us being out of the way, there is nothing [to] impede our progress.

The country is more level than that passed over yesterday in the breaks and ravines of Duck River, and is still of that rich character for soil and natural advantages which has uniformly characterized the country between here and Nashville; but we apparently encamp this evening at the edge of a broken hilly country. Pass Mt. Pleasant ... today.

During today, felt very unwell and ill able to march. Ate nothing after breakfast. Several times during the day did I think I would have to give up and fall behind, and once I got so thoroughly heated up, and worried out, that I would certainly have failed had they not stopped to rest, but I managed to worry through till we reached the camping place, where I set down and rested, went to the branch [stream] near at hand, and washed and cooled off, and finally got into the tent, thoroughly tired out, and sick.

THE DIARY
APRIL ENTRIES

Friday, April 4, 1862

I had hoped we would rest today, but the order to strike tents came early. I had succeeded yesterday morning in getting a small dose of salts as the only medicine they had to give me as a physic [laxative], and which failed to operate. This morning, though I sent for the surgeon, he came not, and I went and crawled into the ambulance and thus started without medicine. Two others got in on the two cots where I lay, and here [we were] jostled and jolted over the rough roads, for we had turned off the pike. I passed the day wearily away, one of those who got in where I lay proceeded to occupy half the cot I lay on (which was only designed for one person) and I could not prevail on him to move until after the middle of the day. When my cramped and straightened position became unbearable, it appeared as if my back would almost break... finally succeeded in getting him to move over and give me the cot.

The "salts" prescribed for Samuel may have been Epsom salts, still used today as a laxative.

Soon after starting, it commenced raining heavily and continued some time, leaking through the cover of the ambulance. When we camp I get into the tent, tired, sore and feeling very badly. The doctor manages to see me this evening and give me a little medicine, [but I am] too unwell to eat.

Saturday, April 5, 1862

Rained smartly again today. Start early this morning. [The] doctor sends me [a] dose of oil which [I] take, then throw up again before we start. Had I got the proper medicine in good time I hardly think I would have been much sick. [I] am handed a ticket and crawl into the

BY THE DIM AND FLARING LAMPS:
THE CIVIL WAR DIARY OF SAMUEL MCILVAINE

ambulance again this morn, where I spend another very disagreeable day. We march steady all day and camp late in the evening.

The nature of the country has changed very materially during the last two days. In fact, we hardly started yesterday morning till we entered a different kind of country; first broken and hilly then it became level and swampy, the roads in many places almost impassable; the timber, a scrubby blackjack, the soil yellow clay; good residences and fine plantations disappear, and log houses and cabins take their places.

Sunday, April 6, 1862

Moderate today.

Start early on our march. I crawl into the ambulance again today feeling quite sick, [have] a fever a good part of the day & night. Spend the day tossing and rolling very uneasily, over rough and bad roads. As I was unable to sit up, I lay at full length, sometimes my head was highest, sometimes my heels, at other times tossed unmercifully from one side to the other.

Pass through Waynsboro [Waynesboro] today, a small and old looking place, but the county seat of the large County of Wayne.

Heavy cannonading was heard at short intervals all day today, south of us, and a little to west. The country passed over today was of much the same character as the two last days, perhaps a shade better; houses and little farms more frequent.

The cannon fire heard by Samuel on the 6th and 7th was likely the Battle of Shiloh, approximately 30 miles south and west of Waynesboro. Gen. Grant described the roar of cannon and small arms as "...the most continous firing of musketry and artillery ever heard on this continent."30

Monday, April 7, 1862

We start very early this morning. Get into the ambulance and pass the day as best I can. The doctors, when they find I am really very sick, manage to visit me and give a good deal of strong medicine, calomel, etc. Stop [this] evening a little before night, in the woods and mud just after crossing Indian Creek.

Calomel (mercurous chloride) was the medical community's preferred cathartic through the 1920s. Unfortunately, calomel had several serious faults -- most significantly, overuse can lead to mercury poisoning. At one point Surgeon General Hammond ordered calomel removed from use because of its hazards; the "calomel rebellion" by military doctors who wanted to prescribe it led to Hammond's removal from his post.31

The country passed over today a good deal similar to that passed yesterday, but I think rather more rolling and hilly; I was so unwell that I paid but little attention to the appearance of the country. I however recollect seeing for the first [time] quite a quantity of large pine timber growing along and over the hills and ridges away from any stream.

---

30 Maj. Gen. U.S. Grant, Letter to Capt. N.H. McLean, in *The War Of The Rebellion: A Compilation Of The Official Records of The Union and Confederate Armies*, Series 1, ed. Lt. Col. Robert N. Scott, (Washington: Government Printing Office, 1882), X, part 1, p. 109.
31 Brooks, pp. 64-65.

BY THE DIM AND FLARING LAMPS:
THE CIVIL WAR DIARY OF SAMUEL MCILVAINE

The roads in many places almost impossible [impassable?] both yesterday and today.

Today again, we hear an almost continuous roaring of cannon, and learn this evening that a battle is raging. The major calls the officers together to consult about an assistant in commanding the regiment as he is the only regimental commander we now have in the regiment, Col. Manson being promoted, and absent on furlough; Col. Kise and the Adjutant being yet under arrest, or at least not allowed to exercise any authority. As they held their consultation near where I still lay in the ambulance, I could hear a part of it. Capt. Hamilton was elected as assistant in the command should they go into battle as they expected to; arrangements were made to leave the sick here, and preparations made to march before day.

Tuesday, April 8, 1862

According to arrangements made last evening, all the sick, and those unable to march were left here; and the regiment [was] up, had breakfast, and [was] on the march long before day. They started with just such of their clothing etc. as they can handily carry, some even leaving their blankets. The teams are to load up and follow at daylight.

A couple of my friends assist me to a hospital tent. It proved to be that of the 4th Kentucky and was pitched on very low ground, surrounded by mud and water. The floor of the tent was literally a mudhole with not a particle of straw or anything of the kind in it. Several sick men were laying in it on cots which lay on the floor in the mud. I spread out a mat (laying in one corner) in the mud & lay down on it. My friends, one of whom was to stay with me, not liking this any better than myself, proposed taking me somewhere else, as there was plenty of room. Nevertheless, they look around (while I am greeted with a chorus of frog music in a pond near the door) and finally find our own hospital tent, and assist me to that, slipping out of the one where I was, while the doctors were out. This [tent] was pitched on rising and dry ground, and they succeeded in getting some cornstalks with the husks and a few blades on them for me to lay on.

I had received during the last few days two or three pretty heavy doses [of] medicine (calomel & bluemass etc.) which operated pretty well, and this evening I feel better, sit up awhile, wash and comb, but the better feeling does not last long; and I go to my hard bed, and lie there with little exceptions until the following Sunday. During the first two or three days & nights it rains considerably, and is very damp and disagreeable. During the first three or four ... days I was there, two or three M.D.'s call at different times and look at me, and give me more strong medicine, bluemass etc. Notwithstanding, my fever was broken, and I assured them over and over my stomach and bowels were out of order, gave me much uneasiness, and that I thought I only needed something to put them in order, and tone up my system, but they seemed to pay no attention to this, and continue [to] give or offer me calomel as the best medicine they have for me, and the only medicine that would do me any good. I made up my mind (especially as my fever was broken) that I had taken quite enough calomel, and therefore declined to take any more, preferring to trust to nature and my naturally good constitution, to bring me around right again, to taking any more strong medicine.

Bluemass was a finely divided preparation of mercury, doubtless prescribed as a cathartic.

I had eaten but little since I took sick, and there [is] nothing provided here for the sick except the hard bread, meat & coffee. However a few potatoes were furnished us, of which the boys made some poor broth (having nothing to season it with). These were soon gone, but the boys finally bought a chicken or two of which to make broth. I could [eat] nothing else, and was so weak I could hardly stand upon my feet a moment when I got upon them.

BY THE DIM AND FLARING LAMPS:
THE CIVIL WAR DIARY OF SAMUEL MCILVAINE

Sunday, April 13th to Friday, April 18, 1862

On Sunday, after being left here I felt considerably better, got up, washed and combed my hair and walked out a few steps. The buds on the trees have swelled & spread into good-sized leaves and now wave in the breeze and begin to form a screen from the rays of the sun. From Sunday on until Friday, the weather being pleasant, I walked around a little each day. I was very weak, and a severe diarrhea now set in on me, and kept me weak. Most of the doctors had gone forward, as well as a good many of the men who were left. We were left under the charge of a steward from the Regulars, who paid little attention to us, except occasionally to come around and deliver some preemptory orders against killing any dogs, sheep etc. to eat (for we were out of rations except crackers, and he furnished us nothing). Had it not been for the kindness of the people in the vicinity (most of whom were Unionists) and that some of us had a little money, we should have fared badly. I ate but little during this week except a little chicken broth, with a little bread (which we bought) in it, and this seemed to run through me like water.

Many of the people around here are very kind to us, and [a] good many of the boys were able to get out, have gone to different places around and are being [kept] free of charge; had I been able, I should have tried before this to find some house to stay at. My friend Peter M. Wiles, who stayed with me to take care of me, [did] the best he could for me, and had it not been for him I know not what I should have done.

Friday, April 18 to Wednesday, April 23, 1862

On Friday the 18th, about two o'clock P.M. a lieutenant of the 1st Ohio Calvary came to the door of our tent, and told us to pack immediately to leave, that they had a team to draw our tents and equipage and ambulances for the sick; accordingly we all packed our things, our tent was struck, our guns, cartridge boxes, knapsacks etc. loaded; as

THE DIARY
APRIL ENTRIES

they came to our tent first, our things were put in the bottom of the wagon.

I had taken some shirts to a house nearby this morning to get washed, and while they [were] packing and loading up I went after them. On getting back, the ambulances were all full, and it was discovered they could neither take all the equipage or all the sick; but they promised to come the next morning for the rest of us.

They had not been gone [long] till a very heavy shower of rain came on; I now was not sorry I did not go with them, although all my things had gone. Saturday [the] 19th [it] rained all day to Sunday [the] 20th and Monday [the] 21st, very nearly all day. Tuesday [the] 22nd was clear and pleasant, also Wednesday [the] 23rd on which day they returned for us, the heavy rains having raised the creeks so that [they] could not cross sooner.

On Friday evening, when I found I was to be left, I applied at the house where I got my shirts washed for privilege to stay overnight, with supper and breakfast, which was granted, although they had refused to take in any of us as boarders. Here I continued to stay until they returned for us nearly a week [later]. Although they were secessionists in principle which they did not deny, and had a son-in-law in the Southern Army, whose wife I saw here every day whilst I stayed with them; yet they used me hospitably while I stayed with them and charged me but $1.50 for the five days.

Whilst here the roses begin to blow [bloom], and other early flowers perfume the air. Here for the first time since leaving home did sleep and rest on a common bed. The first night I had quite a friendly quarrel with the old lady about taking off the featherbed. I had been used to a hard bed so long I thought I would [not] rest well on feathers, and insisted on having it off. She thought it would not hurt me, and refused to take it off. So I started to bed (upstairs) observing if I could not rest on the feathers that I could get up and take them off myself. I therefore went to bed on the feathers, but found them to do so much better than I had expected that I had no occasion to take them off.

Although this family were in good circumstances, owning a large tract of land and several Negroes, yet they had to use rye for their cof-

BY THE DIM AND FLARING LAMPS:
THE CIVIL WAR DIARY OF SAMUEL MCILVAINE

fee, saying they could get none other at all *now*, and the last they bought cost a dollar a pound. This family denied that Unionists here were oppressed, or abused, or pressed into the service of the South, alleging that both ... Wayne, and the adjoining county, Hardin, were strongly Union, and gave large majorities for the Union at the election for the dissolution. They told of a good many living around here who had joined the Union Army to fight against their own country, [who] were no better than dogs, and did not deserve to live. They laid in a good many complaints to me, about the destruction of property fencing in particular by our army as they passed through, for which they expected to get nothing.

In fact, Hardin County was strongly pro-Union, especially in the eastern part of the county. The county had in fact voted against secession in 1861.[32]

I had several arguments, but in a friendly spirit with the old gentleman, in regard to difficulties and their cause, which had plunged this once happy and peaceful country into its present terrible state of Civil War; but in nothing could we agree, save in deprecation of the abrogation of the Missouri Compromise line. I am persuaded I made a favorable impression on this family; when we separated the old gentleman insisted on my taking his name and address "John Bundy, Smith's Fork, Hardin County, Tennessee" and writing to him sometime in the future, promising to answer me. I fared well with this family, began to have a pretty good appetite, and my strength [began] to return.

The Missouri Compromise of 1820 prohibited slavery in parts of the Louisiana Purchase south of 36° 30' latitude;

---

[32] Maj. Gen. U.S. Grant, Letter to Capt. N.H. McLean, in *The War of The Rebellion: A Compilation Of The Official Records of The Union and Confederate Armies*, Series 1, ed. Lt. Col. Robert N. Scott, (Washington: Government Printing Office, 1882), X, part 1, p. 109.

THE DIARY
APRIL ENTRIES

the Kansas-Nebraska Act of 1854 repealed this provision, and played a major role in hastening the outbreak of the Civil War.[33]

Corn planting here had commenced the first of this month, and some of the farmers had got small pieces planted, but the wet weather had effectually stopped the business, and now near the last of the month, there was no [more] planted than at the first of the month. I noticed some of the plows whilst here; they looked as if they belonged to the last century. Much better ones were thrown away in our country when I was a small boy. During our march through this State, although cotton & tobacco houses and sheds for pressing cotton etc. were very frequent, but during our whole march through the State, I never saw anything like, what in *our* country, would be called a barn, a fact perhaps somewhat illustrative of the mildness of the climate. Good meadows were also very rare, and hay seldom seen, the roughness [roughage] commonly used for winter food for stock was corn blades stripped off the stalk and stacked up, or the tops taken off above the ears. Sometimes, though seldom, the whole stalk cut up and put in shock as in our country. I presume not a great deal of roughness [roughage] is needed here for stock, as by a judicious arrangement of pasturage, grass may be had about all winter.

"To put into shock" means to pile the sheaves of grain or stalks of corn in a field with butt ends down.

This seems to be a good country for peaches and during our march south from Nashville, peach bloom has greeted us almost in every fence corner, yet good thrifty apple orchards seem scarce, more to carelessness, than to the want of a good country for raising apples. [I have never seen a country combining so many natural advantages as does that we passed through south of Nashville: timber of an excellent

---

[33] Winthrop D. Jordan, Leon F. Litwack, *et. al.*, p. 327.

BY THE DIM AND FLARING LAMPS:
THE CIVIL WAR DIARY OF SAMUEL MCILVAINE

quality, the richest of soils, an abundance of stone cropping out of the banks on every bend, babbling brooks of pure water, running over rocky beds and ledges, and a most genial climate, combine to make it a most beautiful and delightful country to live in, were it not that the accursed institution of human slavery hangs like a dark pall over this beautiful land.

Wednesday April 23, 1862

About two o'clock P.M. today [they] returned for the balance of us, and we immediately packed up and started for Clifton [Wayne County, Tennessee]. Several left here [who] have [fallen] a sacrifice by disease to their country, but none from our regiment. [Clifton is] a little town on the Tennessee River about nine or ten miles distant, where we arrived about sundown, crossing Indian and Hardin's Creek on the way, and passing over an exceedingly rough, hilly, and rocky road. The prevailing timber [is] a small class of oak, as it is where we have been stopped, with here and there a poplar, and occasionally a little sugartree & beech. We however pass several springs of excellent water, which was a thing we did not find where we were left sick.

Arrived in Clifton. We took up our quarters in a tavern house, which our men had converted into a hospital.

Soon after our arrival, I went to the bank and got my first view of the Tennessee River. It is here smartly larger than the Cumberland at Nashville, and though hardly wider than the Wabash in our country, it is evidently much deeper.

During the last five days, my strength has gradually increased, but so slowly as to be almost imperceptible. My appetite has become good, and I have lost in a measure the disagreeable taste in my mouth. I have also got much better of my diarrhea.

THE DIARY
APRIL ENTRIES

Thursday, April 24, 1862

Warm and pleasant today, pass around town a little today. Make a few little purchases, find almost everything about three [times normal] prices, for instance, common writing paper 60 cents per quire.

A quire of paper is one-twentieth of a ream, or 25 sheets.

An unfortunate accident occurred here today, in the drowning of an Ohio cavalryman, who was bathing and swimming his horse in a little creek nearby but in which the water was deep, being backed up from the river.
Many steamboats are continually passing [up] and down the river, and by night some half dozen round to and land here, putting off forage for the cavalry stationed here, and taking on wagons, mules, horses, and camp equipage, for Pittsburg Landing.

Pittsburg Landing is the town nearest the Battle of Shiloh.

Friday, April 25, 1862

Rained last night; dull, cloudy, and rainy today.
About ten o'clock A.M. we were notified to get ready to go aboard one of the boats at the landing. We therefore pack our things, and a little before twelve midnight go aboard the *Sam'l Gaty* for Pittsburg Landing, and soon after start up the river. On going from the hospital to the boat, I find myself stronger than I had suspected, as I succeeded in carrying my gun, cartridge box, knapsack full [of] clothing, canteen full of water, haversack full of provisions to last us while on the boat, and my carpet sack full of clothing, books, papers, & sundries, alto-

BY THE DIM AND FLARING LAMPS:
THE CIVIL WAR DIARY OF SAMUEL MCILVAINE

gether making quite a considerable load. The distance [is] about 1/4 of a mile and very muddy.

After starting, we continue up five or six miles and stop to take on wood, where we detain until near night; after wooding, proceed up the river, passing Savannah [seat of Hardin County, Tennessee] after dark. Saw a few lights on shore, and several boats at the landing was all I could see to indicate the town.

Saturday, April 26, 1862

Very pleasant this morning.

Our boat had stopped during the night at the lower Pittsburg Landing, but moves up this morning to ... the upper landing some two or three miles [beyond], and commences unloading.

I tried very hard this morning to get something warm for my breakfast, but I could not even buy a cup of coffee. I however bought five apples for as many cents; a treat, not lately enjoyed.

We were put off this morning at the upper landing without a guide or conductor, and left to find our way as best we might to our regiments. After much perplexity and trouble about crossing creeks, hunting roads, etc. in which almost every one I enquired of directed me a different way and in which I got separated from my companions, I finally (near sundown) found my way to our regiment and I hope and trust it may not be my lot to again take sick while on a march.

[At my regiment] I was warmly greeted by my companions. Here I found three or four letters waiting [for] me from friends but ... none from home.

I had a very heavy load to carry. (All my things I carried to the boat yesterday.) I was very tired & weary when I reached camp. Had anyone told me this morn when I started from the river that I could carry my load through to *camp*, I should not have believed him, yet by resting often, I managed to get through with it without other help than that rendered me by a clever young man I fell in with, and who carried

THE DIARY
APRIL ENTRIES

my satchel or carpet sack until his road turned off, a distance of about two miles.

In making our way to the camp, we had a deep creek or bayou to cross. In this the water was backed up from the river until it would swim the horses used in teaming. Whilst sitting here waiting for a chance to cross, I saw several wagons come uncoupled in the middle of the stream, the front wheels and team coming out, but leaving the wagon bed with those in it floating in the middle of the stream. Those who took the precaution to tie down their wagon beds went through safe; a pontoon bridge is being thrown across this creek & will probably be done before night. After sitting here for some time, I finally applied for, and got the privilege of riding across on one of the wagons loaded with hay; it was here I got lost from my comrades & made the rest of the way alone.

The whole country here is or has been one vast encampment, and is cut up with the tracks of the heavy army wagons & roads run in every direction. In hunting the road to my regiment, I heard of the 4th Kentucky and knowing it to be in the same brigade with us, I went to their camp to enquire, but could learning nothing of our regiment, except that they had moved to the advance [a] day or two before; I had hoped to fall in with some wagon returning from the river to camp, in which I could get a chance to ride at least part of the way, but no such good fortune awaited me.

On my way to camp today, I passed over a small part of the upper portion of the battlefield of the 6th & 7th. I saw many trees which had been struck by cannon shot, some of the smaller ones were cut off, other larger ones split open or bored through by cannon balls while the scars of musket balls were on every hand. I passed many mounds of earth where dead men and dead horses were buried, and other places where horses killed in the battle had been burned; the ground here was generally covered with an open woods, with an occasional open field, but some places with a thick growth of underbrush. I was told that [in] some places on the battlefield the underbrush was literally sowed ... with the musket balls, but this part of the field I did not see.

BY THE DIM AND FLARING LAMPS:
THE CIVIL WAR DIARY OF SAMUEL MCILVAINE

The battle of the 6th and 7th was the Battle of Shiloh. Gen. Grant's army had camped at Pittsburg Landing as part of Grant's plan to attack the Memphis and Charleston Railroad; Confederate Gen. A. S. Johnston's army surprised Grant's forces who had not bothered to fortify their encampment. This second great engagement of the Civil War resulted in heavy casualties on both sides and Union victory.

Sunday, April 27, 1862

Clear and exceedingly pleasant today.

Feel the worse [because] of ... yesterday's trip, my back quite weary and lame from carrying so heavy a load yesterday.

Nothing important transpires in camp today. Spend the day in conversation, and in writing to my wife and friends. My comrades who came onto the battlefield on Tuesday evening before the dead were buried, and [the] wounded cared for, gave me some horrifying accounts of the terrible scenes they witnessed there. I received a letter from home this evening in which I am happy to learn my family and friends are well.

On coming up with the regiment, I learn that our brigade, under command of Gen. Fry, a day or two after their arrival at Pittsburg Landing went up the Tennessee River accompanied by a gunboat landed at Chickasaw, just in the corner of Alabama. [They] went out twelve or fifteen miles driving the rebel scouts and pickets before them, destroyed an important bridge on the Memphis and Charleston Railroad across Bear River and one or two others of minor importance, seized a quantity of cotton, press, [and] all the teams they could readily get to draw the cotton to the river. This was considered a daring feat and they were followed to the river by a large rebel force, but too late to molest them. They returned without accident or loss. I was much chagrined that I was unable to be with them, as this is the only important expedition or action our regiment has been engaged in, in which I did not take a part.

"Press" is the compressed and bundled bale of cotton. Denying cotton to the Confederacy was important both because it was necessary for uniforms and because it was a source of foreign exchange for the South; cutting off the supply of cotton made it more difficult for the Confederacy to buy military goods abroad.

Monday, April 28, 1862

Very balmy and pleasant today.
Our regiment go[es] out on picket duty this morning to remain until tomorrow morning. I feel much better today, but thought it not advisable to go out with the pickets this morning. Nothing of importance occurs in camp today. Spend considerable [part] of the day in reading. We get the Cincinnati & Louisville & St. Louis papers here occasionally via the river but they are four or five days old before they reach us. A rumor is going through camp this evening, that our forces have taken Yorktown & New Orleans.

The rumored captures of Yorktown and New Orleans were incorrect. New Orleans was captured May 1st, and Yorktown was captured May 3rd.[34]

Tuesday, April 29, 1862

Rained heavily in the night, but ceases this morning.

---

34 Winthrop D. Jordan, Leon F. Litwack, *et. al.*, pp. 353-354.

BY THE DIM AND FLARING LAMPS:
THE CIVIL WAR DIARY OF SAMUEL MCILVAINE

A rumor comes this morn that our pickets have had a skirmish. Our regiment comes in about noon, but had heard nothing of the rumored fight. Several regiments pass our camp today, moving toward the enemy which I learn are concentrating in great force at Corinth [seat of Alcorn County, Mississippi], about eighteen or twenty miles to the south of us. I still continue slowly to increase in strength. Spend the day in reading, writing and assisting a little with the cooking, etc.

Wednesday, April 30, 1862

Cloudy today and lowery [gloomy in New England dialect].

The rear of our army continues to move out past us, and our camp which had occupied the advance, bids fair to soon be in the rear. Nothing of special importance in camp, except the regular mustering out, and inspection of arms and accouterments, which takes place on the regular payday at the end of each two months.

As all who do not feel fit for duty (to prevent invidious distinctions) are required to get excuses from the Regimental Surgeon, I get an excuse this morning from duty, and also an order or permit to authorize the sutler to sell me some liquor to make bitters of, but the liquor is all out and I fail to get any.

A "sutler" was a private merchant appointed by the Army who sold food and other supplies to soldiers. While many soldiers felt the prices charged were extortionate, these prices reflected dramatically higher risks to the sutler's inventory and losses associated with the severe conditions of being mobile.[35]

---

[35] Billings, pp. 224-228.

May Entries

Thursday, May 1, 1862

Exceedingly pleasant and continues so all day.
Nothing of importance transpires in camp today. I get excused from duty again this morning. The surgeon recommends me a dram of liquor two or three times per day with a little quinine in it [and] authorizes me to come to his office or tent and get it. I spend the day in reading, writing, walking about.

John D. Billings, a Union soldier of the Civil War, described the use of quinine this way: "The proverbial prescription of the average army surgeon was quinine, whether for stomach or bowels, headache or toothache, for a cough or for lameness, rheumatism or fever and ague. Quinine was always and everywhere prescribed with a confidence and freedom which left all other medicines far in the rear".[36]

We receive papers today of the 28th ... from which we learn certainly the capture by the Union forces of New Orleans and Fort Pulaski.

Fort Pulaski, on Cockspur Island, east of Savannah, Georgia, was captured by Union forces April 11th. The loss of this fort was significant both because it enabled a more effective Union blockade of Savannah harbor, and because

---

36 Billings, pp. 175-176.

BY THE DIM AND FLARING LAMPS:
THE CIVIL WAR DIARY OF SAMUEL MCILVAINE

it proved that masonry fortresses were unable to withstand rifled cannon.[37]

As we passed out today, a short distance from our camp, I witnessed a sight I had little thought of ever seeing even on a battlefield. Seeing little mounds of earth scattered through the woods, I approached one and observed a bit of cloth or blanket lying on one end of a pile of dirt. One of my comrades directed me to raise it up. To my horror it disclosed a man's skull, the skin had decomposed and slipped off and his hair lay around his half uncovered skull on the dirt as the rain had beat, or washed it down. Another one's head and face I saw projecting from the slight covering of earth. A third one's whole breast was exposed, and in which the worms were working a speedy destruction. They had just been laid upon the ground upon their blankets or perhaps found there, and [a] little dirt was thrown over them. They were of the enemy ... who fell in the recent battle and were thus buried by their comrades on Sunday night. My feelings were much shocked, and I know not why our officers permitted them to remain thus. I would freely, for humanity's sake, have volunteered to give them a more decent burial had my strength permitted.

In fact, the Union had given them a decent burial, or as decent as the circumstances at the Battle of Shiloh allowed. One soldier described the scene after the battle this way: "In places dead men lay so closely that a person could walk over two acres of land and not step off the bodies."[38] Mass graves "... some more than fifty feet long, six feet wide, and four feet deep, were dug to receive the dead." Union and Confederate troops were buried separately, but both groups

---
37 "Fort Pulaski", *Encyclopedia Americana*, 1963, XI, 514b-514c.
38 John G. Biel, ed., "Notes and Documents: The Battle of Shiloh: From the Letters and Diary of Joseph Demmet Thompson.", Tennessee Historical Quarterly, vol. 27-3, pp. 250-274, quoted in Sword, p. 429.

were sometimes buried two or three deep.39 Heavy rainstorms in mid-April washed away the thin layer of dirt covering the mass graves, causing the macabre sight Samuel describes above.40

Friday, May 2, 1862

Very pleasant today. Read some this morning (news of course). Go [this] eve with my friends, William Holton and Cole H. Campbell (whom I forgot to mention came up with the regiment again two or three days since; the former being left sick at Lebanon, Kentucky, in February; the latter at Columbus [Columbia], Tennessee as we came through there), on a visit to the 14th & 10th Indiana Regiments not far off, but as when hunting the way to my own regiment we had a good deal of trouble to find them. Some of those we enquired of had a kind of indistinct idea of their location, but could give us no definite instruction as to how to find them. After several miles travel in which we circled clear around their camp and came part way back, we at last found them. Spend an hour or two very pleasantly with old acquaintances and associates from our own neighborhood, *viz.* Capt. J. G. Parker, Lts. N. J. Templeton & James Young and others of the 10th. The news current wherever we go [is] of the surrender of Yorktown [Virginia].

This news was premature; Confederate Gen. Joseph E. Johnston didn't retreat from Yorktown, Virginia, until the night of May 3rd, some 24 hours later.41

---

39 Sword, p. 431.
40 Sword, p. 432.
41 Winthrop D. Jordan, Leon F. Litwack, *et. al.*, p. 354.

BY THE DIM AND FLARING LAMPS:
THE CIVIL WAR DIARY OF SAMUEL MCILVAINE

Saturday, May 3, 1862

Somewhat cloudy today. I go with two or three others of our company to a Daguerrean gallery [photographic studio], which is following the army, and get our portraits taken. Having been strongly requested by friends since I entered the army for my likeness, I take this opportunity and get three taken to send to them. I get them taken with my warlike implements on, gun in hand, knapsack strapped on and equipped in marching order.

See plates I and II; plate I was taken before Samuel entered the army; plate II is apparently one of the photographs taken at this point.

On getting back to camp, we find preparations being made for an advance on the morrow toward Corinth. Capt. Van Natta being quite sick is sent to hospital boat at river.

Write this eve to my wife and children; and although the papers & army correspondents are keeping the whole country almost breathless with suspense, by holding up to view the terrible struggle that is soon to take place between the contending armies; yet I cannot bring my mind to believe from various reasons that there is to be another great battle here. I think Beauregard, although boasting to his Government that he had whipped Lincoln's army at Shiloh, and felt able to hold his position at Corinth, against anything we could bring against him, [is] too shrewd a general to risk another general engagement with an army which drove him off the field; and which he must know has been and is being largely reinforced. Notwithstanding, his army may also be increasing, yet I cannot see where he can draw forces [from] ... sufficient to give him a fair prospect of successfully coping with us. These views I write to my family endeavoring to quiet their fears and apprehensions, in regard to another great battle here; reminding them of the terrible and bloody scenes as represented by the papers, which were to take place at Bowling Green, Columbus, and other places, but which were finally evacuated by the enemy without the firing of a gun.

Sunday, May 4, 1862

Cloudy this morning, commences raining about eleven o'clock A.M. and rains all the balance of the day.

Write a few more lines this morning to my wife, and mother, enclosing one of the portraits, and a green leaf from an oak tree (now almost full size) that [she] may compare it with the leaves at home; but on going to deposit my letter find the mail already gone out. I will therefore have to keep it until we get settled in camp again.

Get things ready, strike tents and start about ten o'clock A.M. Soon after starting, it commenced to rain, and as I had said, rained all the balance of the day on us making the roads very muddy and slippery. We pass over a wide, low, flat piece of creek bottom with the creek, which would have been impassable for our wagons, but that our men have corduroyed it with rails, poles, etc. We march today six or eight miles, passing a place consisting of a few scattering houses called Montera. The occupants or owners seem to have all fled and the principal building is now occupied by Gen. Halleck as his headquarters.

Union Gen. Henry Wager Halleck (1815-1872): Halleck, like many other Army officers of the time, enjoyed a successful career outside the military between the Mexican and Civil Wars. After graduating from West Point and fighting in the Mexican War, he served as Secretary of State in the military government of California, helping to write California's state constitution in 1849. Halleck practiced law in San Francisco from 1854 to 1861, when he reentered the army as a major general. Halleck's skills were more administrative than as a field commander, and he was promoted to general in chief of the armies in July, 1862.[42]

I observe on our march today that the telegraph wires are put up as fast as the army advances. As soon as one headquarters is left behind and another selected in advance, the telegraph wire is immediately advanced to the new position, and even branch wires are run to the headquarters of divisions.

Before reaching camp this evening, I fall behind two or three miles from weakness, for the first time since entering the service.

Roads in many places exceedingly bad, [I] pass wagons and ambulances with commissary stores stuck in the mud and left by the enemy. Our wagons with our tents, equipage & provisions do not get up [to our position] tonight. It ceases to rain about dark. Get some brush to put under us (as the ground is covered with pools of water). Spread our oilcloths on poles temporarily fixed over us to keep off the rain as well as possible, and dispose ourselves to rest as well as we may with feet to a good fire of rails. We [are] exceedingly weary, at least on my part.

Monday, May 5, 1862

Passed a very comfortable night. It commenced raining again about eleven or twelve o'clock in the night, rained pretty hard, bagging the oilcloths down till they would catch nearly a pailful of water, when they would give way and let it pour through upon us. Beside [which] it rained upon our feet and heads around the edges, but finally morning came, the blankets over us as well as the clothes upon our persons were completely saturated, and the water stood in pools under us, and had drowned our fire entirely out. It continues to rain this morning until about ten o'clock.

A squad of men was sent from each company back to assist the teams up, which began finally to arrive. Our[s] came about eleven

---

[42] "Halleck, Henry Wager", *Encyclopedia Americana*, 1963, XIII, 646-647.

THE DIARY
MAY ENTRIES

o'clock A.M. or nearly so late. It would have been amusing to a looker on, this morning to see us standing around our campfires in the rain, boiling sassafras tea in our tin cups, our cooking vessels all back with the wagons. Fortunately we were camped in an old field where there was plenty of young sassafrass roots easily obtained, with which we made tea which answered an excellent purpose -- notwithstanding, our facilities for making it were none of the best. I was also lucky enough to get a little coffee which one of our men had brought along, and boiling it in my tin cup, had a good cup of coffee.

About eleven o'clock A.M. the sun comes out and shines very warm, giving us a chance to dry our wet clothing, books, papers, etc. We get our tent up, and I carry several pails of water which stood in puddles within. It is said that, "Necessity is the mother of invention" and we feeling disinclined to sleep on the damp ground; set to work to remedy the difficulty, and soon fix up little cots or beds, [made] of poles a foot or so from the ground, upon which we spread fine brush and leaves, thus fixing pretty comfortable beds.

We get a paper today of the first ... in which the taking of New Orleans by our troops is confirmed, but the surrender of Yorktown is not mentioned and appears to have been a false report.

I have felt quite unwell all day, diarrhea returning on me. Get [up], and take some medicine for it this evening.

Tuesday, May 6, 1862

Sun rises clear and pleasant this morning.

Camp guards are mounted again this morning, none having been on since we moved. Mailed the letter written two days since to my wife. Gets quite warm. Nothing of importance transpires in camp today, except the reading of an order on dress parade this evening (which I attend for the first time since coming up) notifying us that Gen. Sherman is now our Division Commander. Many rumors are afloat in camp. The evacuation of Corinth by the enemy continues to be rumored.

BY THE DIM AND FLARING LAMPS:
THE CIVIL WAR DIARY OF SAMUEL MCILVAINE

Wednesday, May 7, 1862

Quite cool through the night; clear and pleasant today.

Two more of our company come up with us today, Dr. Killin and J. Doloban, who were left at Mill Spring and have since been home on furlough. The day passes off much as usual in camp, except that there was something of a bustle created this evening at dress parade by the reading of an order to prepare and keep on hand ten days' rations, and all the tents except two to each company were to be sent back to the river and turned over to the quartermaster; each man to carry in his cartridge box 40 rounds of cartridges, and 60 additional on his person, and to be always ready to march at a moment's notice. This looks a good deal like fighting was expected.

Thursday, May 8, 1862

Cool again last night, but quite warm through the day today.

A call on our regiment to go on picket at two o'clock [P.M.]; but on getting ready and getting into line, the order is countermanded, in consequence of several divisions being already in our advance. Rumors continue to flow in of the evacuation of Corinth. A paper of the [fifth] ... [is] received which gives rumors of it from rebel papers. Capt. Van Natta returns this evening improved in health, and is joyfully greeted by the company. Several more doctors also arrive from Indiana in anticipation of the coming battle, among them Dr. Messner formerly of Pine Village, Warren County, but now Co. [probably Company] Treasurer, with whom I have some conversation. Write some this evening.

Friday, May 9, 1862

Rather cloudy but pleasant today.

THE DIARY
MAY ENTRIES

A general review and inspection of arms, etc. by Gen. Sherman of his whole division today. More doctors arrive this evening, everything goes to prove that the Northwestern States are intensely excited, and in breathless suspense at the prospect of the coming conflict here. Cannonading heard this evening again in the direction of Corinth.

The "Northwestern States" of Samuel's time would be called the Midwest today.

I have felt quite unwell today, and yesterday ... diarrhea having returned upon me again with severe gripping pains. Get it checked smartly today. Feel too unwell to write, consequently my letter begun yesterday has to lay over. The [water?] here as everywhere else [we] have camped this side [of] the river is miserably poor stuff.

Saturday, May 10, 1862

Very warm today.
Orders were received about ten o'clock this morning, to be ready to march in half an hour. I at first conclude not to go, in consequence of feeling so unwell, but on learning we would not move over two miles, I decide to go and get necessary amount of cartridges to make out my 100, and a few hard crackers, and a small piece of fat meat. Finally after being called into line, and standing half an hour, move some two hundred yards and stand another half hour.
I go to a well at a house nearby to get my canteen filled, find it so crowded that men were offering five to ten cents to get their canteens filled. Watching my opportunity, I get hold of a pole they were drawing with, fastening my canteen with several others to it, let them down and succeed in filling them.
We move up a little farther, stop again, all this time the hot sun pouring down upon us. Finally Col. [A.O.] Miller gets a chance and moves us up into the edge of the timber, where we wait an hour or two

more (but now in the shade) for the privilege of the road. We move about two miles out on a very winding course and stop but little before dark, so tedious were our movements. Our wagons fail to come up, and we sleep in the open air but comfortably, as the weather is pleasant.

Sunday, May 11, 1862

Very warm again today.

A rather singular death occurred in Company I of our regiment this morning. A little before day, two or three loose horses came rushing through the quarters & among the sleeping men, passing near where this man, H. Osborne, lay. Most of us nearby were aroused and raised partially up, this man with the rest. Several hallowed as if scared, some of them hallowing [that] the rebels were upon us, but the horses passed on, and all lay down again. At daylight, or some half an hour afterward, this man was found dead.

Our whole brigade go out on picket about seven or eight o'clock [P.M.] I remain in camp. The wagons come up early, and return to [our] old camp for balance of our things, notwithstanding the recent order to send our tents to the river, all were brought forward and pitched again.

The officers [are] at work yesterday morning and today on payrolls.

[The sky] indicates rain pretty strongly but passes without and our men on picket fare well as to the weather. Spend the day in reading.

Monday, May 12, 1862

The sun rises clear and pleasant, gets quite warm during the day.

About two o'clock [P.M.] men come in off picket much heated up, and covered with sweat and dust. They report no difficulty, but had an alarm driving in their pickets. This brought us within about three miles of Corinth (as represented on a guide board [sign post]) and within two [miles] of the enemy's fortifications. Coming to a large open

THE DIARY
MAY ENTRIES

field of 1/2 mile or more across it, we formed a line of battle, and owing to some irregularity [of] the movements, most of the right wing of our regiment were thrown behind, and had to double quick it most of the way across the field in order to catch up with the left, and the other regiments in the line which also went at a very quick step. In this we got very much heated up (the sun now shining very hot) and nearly exhausted. Some of them did give out and fall back, but I was able to maintain my position in the line. After marching across the field and a narrow strip of timber into the edge of another field driving the rebel pickets before us, we halted, and fell back again into the strip of timber, rested awhile, and returned to camp.

We had hardly cooled off, till the order came to prepare one day's rations and get ready to go on picket. This done we started, and as I had stood pretty well through the day, and there appeared a fair chance for some excitement, after driving in the enemy's pickets [earlier], I determine to go out with them; ... [I] started, on getting out about one mile [we] were halted to make arrangements.

While waiting, I had occasion to step aside to attend to a call of nature, the regiment soon moved forward, the right wing taking a right, and the left, a left-hand road. I soon followed, but was told by some of our cavalry that they had stopped nearby. I concluded to stop at a house and replenish my canteen of water; taking their track I followed on. After [this I] found they had gone about a mile farther.

On reaching the edge of the field where we had formed our line of battle this morning, I heard a brisk firing ahead and supposed the enemy had engaged our men. I hurried on across this field double quick again, but after fifteen or twenty shots the firing ceased.

On reaching the other side of the field, I met three of our cavalrymen coming from toward the enemy's lines. They seemed considerably excited, and one of them had his hat. They told me they had [gone] beyond our picket line to see what they could see, and the enemy had fired on them, and that our regiment stationed in the narrow woods, ... supposing a large force of the enemy were about to charge on them, had left taking the road around the field to the right. They said they were scared off, which I could not very well deny or disbelieve, as I saw

BY THE DIM AND FLARING LAMPS:
THE CIVIL WAR DIARY OF SAMUEL MCILVAINE

their blankets, haversacks, etc. lying in a line where they had apparently very hurriedly left them.

The expression "had his hat" clearly had some idiomatic meaning, perhaps indicating fear or excitement; I am unable to determine at this late date what Samuel meant.

The cavalry men pointed me to a rebel horseman standing in the road on a rising ground about three hundred yards from where we stood. He was apparently watching our movements. They also said if I would go over the rise a little I could see plenty more of them, but I had no particular inclination to go much farther in that direction just at the present. I doubt not I could have moved up among the trees and brush sufficiently near to have shot the horseman I saw in the road, but I had no particular inclination to draw a party of enemy's cavalry after me, although I might possibly have dodged them in the brush.

After hearing what the three men had to say, and having no idea how far back our men had fallen, I thought it most prudent to leave, and as I had some open ground to pass over before the brush would shelter me from view, I made some tolerably quick steps. Had I not been so fortunate as to meet with the three men, or had my attention arrested by our men's blankets etc. I would undoubtedly have [gone] so near the enemy before discovering my mistake, that I would have been taken prisoner.

Taking the course pointed out by the cavalrymen, I followed on, and in about 1/2 mile [found] some of our officers stationing a new line of pickets. I passed on and finally overtook our company near the house I stopped at to get water. After reading my tramp [reciting my hike], and how I had followed them around, alone, saw their blankets, haversacks, etc. where they left them in their fright, and came off unmolested, we had a hearty laugh over the ludicrous circumstance. They [the cavalrymen] excused their conduct by saying that soon after stopping and laying off their blankets, etc., the firing was done just over the rise from them. Here they were order[ed] to fall back a little

& take position behind a fence. [Then] some of our cavalry came rushing, saying a large force of the enemy were approaching & they would be cut off, hereupon they were ordered to fall back or retreat, and had no opportunity to recover their blankets. I afterward understood our men had [gone] out farther than they were ordered to go through some mistake.

Our company were stationed for the night near where I overtook them, whilst others were thrown out in advance to the edge of the large field already mentioned as having been crossed two or three times today.

Friday, May 16, 1862

The night was pleasant, followed by another warm day.

I sit up till midnight, on a log near the roadside. When I was relieved, and [I] lay down under some bushes to sleep, but slept very little. There was such a continual firing kept up all night among the advance pickets that I could not sleep. Most of the firing was off to our right where our line was occupied by Illinois troops & cavalry. Once near midnight quite a heavy volley was fired. I cannot learn this morning that anything was affected in the night by the continuous firing, and think most of it was premature and useless.

It was reported over and over by cavalrymen & others this morning that the enemy had occupied the ground we had left last evening, but this was found to be a false report, as our men ventured back this morning [and] recovered their blankets, oilcloths, etc. Some had even left their haversacks, with their provisions in them. Perhaps the want of a breakfast stimulated them to make an effort to recover them.

After we got breakfast, (making coffee in our tin cups, and broiling our meat on the coals of [the] fire), we advanced again and occupied the ground left last night. Soon we hear considerable firing along the advance picket lines, and are several times called to arms, expecting an advance of the enemy in force to recover their lost ground. Had they

BY THE DIM AND FLARING LAMPS:
THE CIVIL WAR DIARY OF SAMUEL MCILVAINE

[come] we were prepared for them, having a strong reserve in the rear of our pickets.

About ten o'clock A.M. the enemy sent ... something over 100 of their prisoners under a flag of truce to exchange; they (the prisoners) represent that food is very scarce in the rebel Army, that they had been kept on about half rations, and that their meat was mule meat, etc.

Again this evening, we hear a brisk firing off to our right which is kept up for some time. Finally we are relieved and return to camp. We could plainly and distinctly, as if but a little way off, hear the enemy's drums, both this morning and evening from our picket stand, as well as the whistle of the locomotive on the railroad running into and out of Corinth, all of which does not indicate very *strongly* that they have yet left. I take a regular bath and wash off all over this evening.

Saturday, May 17, 1862

A very fine morning.

Get an order early to [be] ready to move at eight o'clock [A.M.], with two days' rations. Our tents were struck and camp equipage loaded. We marched over the same ground this morning [we] passed over yesterday and day before. [We] took up a position some distance in advance of that occupied yesterday, left our knapsacks under a guard, [and] moved forward in line of battle, frequently changing our position and maneuvering in the edge of the timber near the other edge of the woods. Company E of our regiment and other companies from different regiments were sent out as skirmishers, while the main body of our forces rested on our arms in the edge of the woods, as a reserve. By night, our men were in possession of about half of the open ground.

When we left our knapsacks ... and advanced, I supposed, and I think it was the general impression, that we were going out to have a fight. In this Col. Kise (who was with us but still dispossessed of his command) seemed to coincide as he rode along the lines, cheering and encouraging the boys, laughingly telling them that if they [did] as well as they did at Mill Spring, the whole regiment would be court-martialed.

Col. Kise refers here to his own court-martial after the Union victory at the Battle of Mill Spring, apparently because his report of the regiment's part in the battle was thought by his superiors to be false.

The teams did not come up this evening, I suppose having orders to remain back. Near nightfall, we changed our position somewhat to the left, and lay on our arms near the picket line, which occupied the edge of the woods.

Sunday, May 18, 1862

Cloudy and cool enough to be pleasant today.

Our teams come up this morning and we clear off the brush and pitch our tents near the position we occupied last night; had hardly [got] them up until an order came to change our position a little to the rear. Put up our tents again, and are cleaning off our guns etc. when the enemy discharged three or four shots from a field piece which they appeared to have brought out near the farther edge of the open field before mentioned. One of them, a canister shot, was discharged among our skirmishers in the field. The iron hail rained among them, and bounding, struck one of our men [of] Company K, severely injuring his hip, but fortunately the shell did not explode. These entrenchments were commenced yesterday, and run a little in front of our camp, between us and the open field.

I went down two or three times to the edge of the disputed field, where our men were skirmishing, to witness their operations, and standing with many others crowded along the fence, we formed a conspicuous mark for the enemy to shoot at, had it not been rather a long shot, yet we could [hear?] their bullets strike the fence, as they shot at

BY THE DIM AND FLARING LAMPS:
THE CIVIL WAR DIARY OF SAMUEL MCILVAINE

some of our men in a clump of brush not far from us. Had they discharged one of their field pieces loaded with canister at us, they would have scattered us in a hurry.

I went down some little distance into this field, once to get water, which is here very scarce and hard to get, the men digging holes along the drains from which they get a little muddy water.

It is astonishing to see the temerity of our men as they walk fearlessly over the open field from point to point, exposing themselves to the shots of the enemy, while the rebels keep concealed behind the fences in the edge of the timber, and in a large orchard on the other side of the field. We could see the flash and smoke of their guns from behind the fencing & in the orchard, but rarely could we get a sight of one of them.

Monday, May 19, 1862

Warm again today.

Take a stroll along the breastworks this morning to our right. They appear to extend the whole length of our line, which according to the best information I can get forms a kind of semicircle around Corinth on the north, the northwest & northeast, about three miles from the town, and are perhaps ten to twelve miles long. They were only commenced day before yesterday and appear to [be] completed or very nearly so, each regiment throwing up works in front of their own camp. The men have been engaged upon them day and night since they commenced. There are frequent angles on the rising ground where arrangements are made to plant batteries. Some of them [are] designed for heavy siege guns.

In the course of my walk, I find myself in the vicinity of the 15th Iowa Regiment, and as Capt. James Seevers [commander, Company C] of that regiment & of Oskaloose, Iowa, married one of my cousins, hunted him up, and made his acquaintance.

On returning to camp find the tents struck and everything ready to move again. Learn that while gone I missed a treat. His Excellency

Gov. Morton had visited the regiment made a few brief remarks to them, stating that he was here to see after the welfare of Indiana soldiers, fill official vacancies, etc. I regret much that I missed seeing and hearing this noble-hearted man.

Indiana Gov. Oliver Perry Morton (1823-1877): A lawyer and circuit judge before the Civil War, he was elected lieutenant governor in 1860. He became governor in 1861 when Gov. Henry S. Lane was elected to the U. S. Senate.[43]

It is not surprising that an Indiana soldier would have such a positive view of Gov. Morton. At one point Indiana troops were ordered to the West Virginia mountains but the quartermasters had failed to provide overcoats. After failing in his efforts to get "his" troops supplied by the Army, Gov. Morton purchased the needed overcoats himself and persuaded the Army to take over the contracts.[44]

After considerable delay and trouble in moving our things from one place to another several times (which we [do] by carrying them), we finally get settled down and our tents pitched again, 300 or 400 yards to the right of our old position and immediately on the line of the breastworks. There is almost continual skirmishing kept each day and most of the night, but without any very serious effects, yet we occasionally hear of a man being shot.

After pitching our tents, our regiment began preparations to go on picket, and go out a little before night, taking their station but 300 or 400 yards in advance of our camp, one company going out as viadetts a little farther.

---

[43] Boatner, p. 571.
[44] Catton, p. 115-116.

BY THE DIM AND FLARING LAMPS:
THE CIVIL WAR DIARY OF SAMUEL MCILVAINE

From the context, "viadett" seems to mean "advance guard", but I was unable to find any proper definition of this word.

Learning from a young man of our regiment and from my neighborhood who has just got a discharge from the service that he is going to start home in the morning, commence writing a letter to my family to send by him, but feeling quite unwell do not finish it.

Tuesday, May 20, 1862

Rained last night... toward day, or rather poured down for a while. Cloudy today but warm.

Essay [attempt] to finish my letter this morning, but before I get it done, I learn the young man is already gone.

Felt so unwell yesterday evening that I did not go out with the regiment and feel still worse today, probably partially from the effects of a dose of medicine taken this morning.

Skirmishing and a continual firing going on a little to our left this morning, quite briskly for awhile; the enemy also throw a few more shells from a battery, or gun, [which] appears to be rather inconveniently near us, one of which lit [landed] in the camp of the 18th Regulars a little to our left, passing through one of their tents and a pile of blankets but without other damage as it did not explode. I have been considerably surprised at our officers in pitching our camps so near the enemy's lines.

Our men come in off picket this evening and report no one hurt.

Rains a little this evening. The rain of last night and this evening will make water more easily obtained, [even] if it did soak our men while on picket duty.

I have felt very unwell all day.

THE DIARY
MAY ENTRIES

Wednesday, May 21, 1862

Cloudy this morning, but clears off and becomes quite warm toward evening. Some very heavy skirmishing today, and from reports brought in, several of our men were killed, though none of our regiment, and a good many wounded.

Our regiment ordered early to get ready with two days' rations to move. At eight o'clock [A.M. we] were called into line, but did not move until near noon; when they went out in advance of the entrenchments, considerably to the right, and made a new encampment, to which they moved all the camp equipage.

Col. Kise, after being so long deprived of his command, took command of the regiment again this morning.

Had the pleasure of seeing Gov. Morton as he rode along the lines this morning with [Brig.] Gen. [Mahlon D.] Manson & others; think it not improbable that one of the good things he [did] was to use his authority and influence in reinstating Col. Kise in his command.

Among those who were wounded today, [were] Lts. Johnson and Shoemake of our regiment, the former receiving a ball through the fleshy part of the arm, the latter wounded in the thigh, but nearly [all the rest] of them seriously. I learn one of them was shot while skirmishing by one of the rebel sharpshooters who was in a tree. Our men discovered him, fired a volley at him which tumbled him out of the tree, and his friends bore him off dead, but our men rushed up in time to capture his gun, a long range rifle with globe sights.

There was a very heavy cannonading a distance on our right lasting however but a short time, and it is reported this evening that Gen. Schoepf captured 300 to 500 prisoners.

This incident is commonly known as the skirmish at Widow Serratt's.

I have felt very unwell all day, was examined by one of the doctors this morning and sent to the Regimental Hospital, [and] kept in a va-

BY THE DIM AND FLARING LAMPS:
THE CIVIL WAR DIARY OF SAMUEL MCILVAINE

cated house a little to the rear of our lines. Here I went about noon, Sgt. A. Cowgill of our company being sent with me. After my arrival there, [I] was examined by another doctor and ordered a dose of medicine to operate on the bowels. [I] had fever and a severe headache.

Thursday, May 22, 1862

Considerably cloudy today.

Sharp skirmishing this morning just before day, a little to our right; twice were our regiment called into line, as some of the boys who visited us inform us. They also inform us that they commenced throwing up a second line of entrenchments, 200 or 300 yards in advance of the first this morning, their part of which was completed before night. Since morning there has been no fighting or skirmishing along our part of the line, although heavy firing was heard far to the left.

Many reports and rumors are in circulation today, although the most worthy one of credence is that our army are in possession of Richmond, others are to the effect that Gen. Butler has taken Jackson, Mississippi, that Beauregard is evacuating or has evacuated Corinth, and that Gen. Siegel or some other general has taken the railroad south of Corinth etc., etc.

Gen. Beauregard in fact evacuated Corinth during the night of May 29-30.[45]

Take a pretty heavy course of medicine, calomel, quinine, capsicum.

---

[45] Long, p. 218.

Capsicum fructescens, a member of the potato family, was used as a gastric and intestinal stimulant.

Friday, May 23, 1862

Cloudy this morning; sets in to raining about nine or ten o'clock and rains pretty nearly all the balance of the day.

No fighting or skirmishing today so far as I hear of along our part of the line or within hearing. I was quite sick again today, a slight chill this morning and fever this evening, so much so that I could not eat anything.

It is remarked on all hands that nothing is heard of the [railroad] cars at Corinth since yesterday morning. And the rebel drums, which have hitherto been regularly heard, are now but slightly distinguishable; what this betokens remains to be seen yet.

Saturday, May 24, 1862

Cool and cloudy today but no rain.

About seven o'clock [A.M.] we (*i.e.* the sick in the hospital) were examined by the Regimental Surgeon, and those who it was thought would not soon be fit for duty are ordered to the hospital boat at the river. I insisted strongly on remaining, thinking that I would be able in a few days to be about again, and would be able at least to stand in the ranks and fight, if it should be necessary (and a battle was now thought to be imminent every day), [but] they wanted the hospital house cleared of the sick to make room for the wounded. My entreaties to be left were unavailing, the order to go to the boat was preemptory [mandatory], and I had to acquiesce.

We were to go in the wagons that were going to the river for forage and provisions, and bade to get ready and be off immediately. Most of my things were at the camp; there was no one there to go after them and I was unable. My writing material was all left, with my journal,

BY THE DIM AND FLARING LAMPS:
THE CIVIL WAR DIARY OF SAMUEL MCILVAINE

letters, etc. and about half my clothing, but I happened to have with me my memorandum, in which I had [daily] taken notes.

Up to the time we started, there was no change along the lines from yesterday so far as I could learn. Although I had all along been of the opinion, and maintained it among my comrades that we would not have a battle here, I had by this time almost changed my opinion and began to think we would have to fight after all.

Got into one of the rough jolting army wagons with six or eight others to ride to the river a distance of about twenty miles. I knew not how I should stand it but there was no other alternative. Soon after starting, I began to feel chilly and afterward a fever came on; the jolting of the wagon over the rough roads set my head to aching terribly, and long before we reached the river I thought it would almost burst. The roads were rough and made more so by frequent corduroying with rails and poles sometimes for a distance of half a mile, in other places cut out anew among the brush leaving the road full of small stumps.

Arrived about three or four o'clock [P.M.] at Hamburg on the river above Pittsburg Landing (a collection of about a dozen houses) and went aboard the *W. W. Crawford* hospital boat, chartered by the State of Indiana, to carry sick and wounded soldiers. I got to one of the cots prepared for the sick by the kindly assistance of the boat's clerk, for I was scarce able to help myself, and gladly lay down. I had been obliged to sit up all the way in the wagon, sometimes to stand, and was made as comfortable as possible.

The boat soon after started down (but so sick was I that I knew not of its turning downstream, and thought it was going up), stopping at various points until we reached Pittsburg Landing. Here we were reexamined, and about six out of about 28 or 30 of our regiment who came to the river were left at the hospital boat stationed here, [and] the balance were sent down the river. Here it was my fortune to be sent with those that were to go down the river. Dr. Allen, our regimental surgeon [was] along on this examination. When they came to me, [he] said I must go, observing to the other surgeon that I had been one of the best soldiers in the regiment until I broke down. I thought it of no use to interpose any farther objections, and so let them [take] their course with me. In fact I was too sick just now to make much objections to anything. My head continued to ache yet without abating in the least, and I had a hot fever. The boat tied up here for the night. I received no medicine today, nor ate anything.

Sunday, May 25, 1862

Moderate today.

Start early down the Tennessee River, destined as I learned for Evansville, Indiana, and we were told by the doctor in charge of us that on arriving at Evansville, all who were able to ride in the [railroad] cars would be immediately furloughed home for a short time to recruit [recover] our health among our friends.

The day wore away heavily till evening to *me*, for I was unable to be up. My head had continued to ache all night without abating, entirely depriving me of any rest, and not until near noon today did it cease aching. I thought I had had the headache frequently before, pretty severely, but never had I had such a scourge of it as this was; it had lasted without any intermission and that in the severest manner for nearly 30 hours. I was kindly, and attentively, waited on by the attending physician, who this morning had me taken up into one of the staterooms on account of the noise and jarring of the machinery below.

Toward noon, I began to feel better, and finally my curiosity and desire to see what was to be seen getting the better of my sickness, I got up and looked a little. We passed a railroad bridge, nothing of which was left but the piers and draw. This was the railroad from Nashville to Paris, [Tennessee].

I lay down again, being too unwell to remain up, and thus unconsciously passed Fort Henry. I had intended to get up again in time to see it, but was not aware we were so near it. I was much vexed at this disappointment. There was little worthy of note to be seen on the passage down this river. As I learned from others, [there was] once in awhile a desolate looking house on the bank. Soon after passing Fort Henry, night closed in and I went to sleep.

BY THE DIM AND FLARING LAMPS:
THE CIVIL WAR DIARY OF SAMUEL MCILVAINE

Monday, May 26, 1862

Very pleasant today.

On getting up this morning we find our boat tied up at Cairo, and we learn that our boat will go down the Mississippi hunting up the sick, as far as our forces at Fort Pillow.

Considerable trouble experienced in getting coal for the trip this morning, and we run up as far as Mound City [seat of Pulaski County, Illinois], about three or four miles above Cairo [county seat of Alexander County, Illinois] on the Ohio, trying to get it, but without success. Nearly all the coal along here is bought up by the Government for the use of the naval fleets. Returning to Cairo we finally succeed in getting coal.

While the boat is coaling I go ashore, [and] find the townsite to be but little better than a mudhole. The houses are scattered over a considerable space of ground, but are nearly all inferior unpainted wooden buildings. There are just one or two good buildings in the place. The St. Charles Hotel, standing at the extreme point of land between the Ohio & Mississippi (so much so that when the rivers are high the water backs into its cellar) is the only really good building in the place, it is a large and as yet unfinished brick.

Along the railroad track (which runs along the bank of the Ohio for some distance), and which answers the double purpose of railroad track and levee, to keep the river from overflowing the town, is the only dry ground here, at least at the present time; water is yet standing in ponds in the town, and the mud in the streets is just beginning to dry up and get passable.

Mound City is a far dryer, and much better site for a city. It has also located in it a U.S. General Hospital, a large and very fine brick building, now apparently full of sick or wounded soldiers.

Everything around Cairo indicates a recent heavy flood; great numbers of old boats and rivercraft have been floated out of the river, and are left high and dry on the shore. While on shore here, I bought three or four little apples, but was too sick to eat more than 1/2 of one of them. I also felt anxious to read the news again and bought a paper of the 24th ... but it had but little news.

A place rejoicing in the lofty sobriquet [fanciful name] of Ohio City is immediately across the Mississippi from here, but consists of nothing but a small collection of board huts so far as I was able to see.

After getting our coal on, we started and soon passed out into the broad Mississippi, "The Father of Waters". Pass Columbus, [Hickman County] Kentucky, a little before night. The river here is comparatively narrow, with a steep bluff bank on the Columbus or Kentucky side. Some 30 to 40 feet above the present river, I also noticed several places 1/2 way down the bank where terraces were constructed and cannon had been planted. The town appeared to be a small old & dilapidated looking place. Soon after passing Columbus, night came on, and it became too dark to see.

Have felt very unwell today, but better than yesterday; have been able to be up considerably, but unable to eat from sickness at stomach.

Tuesday, May 27, 1862

Morning pleasant, and day warm. Find ourselves tied up at New Madrid [seat of New Madrid County, Missouri] this morning having passed Island No. 10 in the night. This is [a] forsaken and worn out old looking old town, although a county seat. I learn many of the houses have been destroyed since the war began; it is a fine situation for a town, and looks as if the country back [of it] was good. At this place are situated the Indiana 34th Regiment.

Pass on down to Tiptonsville [Tiptonville, seat of Lake County, Tennessee] (a mere landing place), leaving notice at each of these places to have their sick ready by our return. Here are stationed the 47th Indiana.

We pass on down to Fort Pillow, or to the encampment of our forces just above. Here we find the 43rd & 46th Indiana Regiments under command of Col. [Graham N.] Fitch of Logansport, Indiana, who will

BY THE DIM AND FLARING LAMPS:
THE CIVIL WAR DIARY OF SAMUEL MCILVAINE

be recollected by many as one of the so called "bogus senators" from Indiana.

Until 1913, U. S. senators were elected by the state legislatures, not the people. In 1857, the lower house of the Indiana state legislature was controlled by the Democrats; the Republicans controlled the state senate. Since the Democrats constituted a majority of the two houses, the Republicans refused to allow the state senate to go into joint session. The Democrats in the lower house of the state legislature went ahead and elected Fitch and Jesse Bright as U. S. senators without the state senate. Fitch and Bright were eventually accredited as senators from Indiana by the U. S. Senate after a year-long credentials fight.[46]

Fitch was military commander of Memphis after its capture.[47]

But little, except the broad and majestic river with its numerous islands, sand banks, and bars, with an occasional old house, and open or cleared field on the banks is to be seen, all else is shut out from the view by the dense bottom, timber, willows etc. [which] lines the banks.

After stopping I got ashore, determined to make footsteps on the State of Arkansas, [even] if they *were* but few. Walked out a little way from the river, the ground being next [to] the river almost miry. Saw the tents of our men in an old field, and here I saw the first levee I had noticed along the river, which are grown up along the lower Mississippi for the protection of the plantations, and even cities on its bank.

---

[46] Emma Lou Thornbrough, *Indiana in the Civil War Era 1850-1880*, (Indianapolis: Indiana Historical Bureau & Indiana Historical Society, 1965), p. 78.
[47] Thornbrough, p. 149.

THE DIARY
MAY ENTRIES

The levee here was raised about six feet high, and was about wide enough on the top to drive a team & wagon. The soil here seemed exceedingly rich, and although there were some oak trees, the larger part of the timber was cottonwood, and sycamore, some very large ones.

Our mortar boats from a mile or so below were throwing an occasional shell at the enemy, who had been keeping up a pretty vigorous firing on our fleet during the day. There seemed to be considerable objection on the part of the commander here to the objects of our mission, and we learned we would have to stay till morning.

Incredible as it may seem, many military commanders of the Civil War viewed medical care for the sick or wounded as unnecessary.

Felt better today; the sickness at my stomach measurably gone, and I begin to feel a little like eating.

Tuesday, May 28, 1862

Gets quite warm today.

We get but a dozen or so of sick here, out of about 60, whom we learn by many of their officers should by right come.

There are several transport steamers here, some of them along shore, others apparently anchored out at different points along the river. The *Conestoga* gunboat lies at anchor, across a low sandy island from us near the other side of the river. Our line of gunboats and mortars can be distinguished by their smoke something like 1 1/2 miles below. As we start off, a heavy smoke is seen to arise in volume from the rebel fleet, across a point of timber projecting out into a bend of the river, and it is thought they are preparing to make an attack on our fleet. As we pass up, the same monotonous view of sandy islands, sand bars, and bank, and dense bottom timber meets the view with scarce a variation.

BY THE DIM AND FLARING LAMPS:
THE CIVIL WAR DIARY OF SAMUEL MCILVAINE

The *Conestoga* was one of three riverboats converted to gunboats early in the war, while awaiting construction of ironclads more appropriate to river warfare.[48]

At Island No. 18, which is quite a large island, we take on four or five poor families with their effects. They seem determined to leave these uncongenial "diggins" for a more peaceful situation in the North. A few miles farther up, we are flagged by another encampment of refugees, but as they wish is to bring a yoke of oxen, and cow aboard in addition to themselves, we cannot fetch them.

Feel still a little better today. Sit up all day; my appetite increases also.

Thursday, May 29, 1862

A very pleasant day.

Find ourselves hitched up this morning at New Madrid, but I was awakened in the night by the stopping of the boat at Tiptonville to take on some sick.

Have an opportunity while the sick are being fetched on board to see the fortifications from the boat. There is a magazine here, and several batteries of heavy guns, as well as entrenchments for riflemen partly formed with bags of sand. These fortifications were all made by the rebels.

Finally getting ready [to] pass up, have an excellent chance to view Island No. 10 as we pass it about noon. The island, I am informed, contains about 150 acres, is high and dry, and by great odds, the prettiest little island I have seen on the river, being situated in the sharp curve. It has an excellent command of the river both up and down. The Kentucky bank is high and dry and circling around the curve on

---
48 Long, p. 108.

131

this bank, as well as on the island, the rebels had their batteries planted. Our troops have removed the guns [which were] all ... burned on the taking of the place by our forces.

I was also shown the spot where our gunboat fleet walked out of the woods into the river below the island, to the astonishment and dismay of the rebels. The left bank of the river here is low & flat and runs out into a sand bar. On the right bank of the river opposite, and for a mile or two below this island, is the only place on the banks of the Mississippi which I have seen, that looks like a desirable or comfortable place to live.

The Siege of Island No. 10 was the first battle of the Union campaign to gain control of the Mississippi. Island No. 10 no longer exists; the Mississippi has washed it away.[49]

Pass Hickman [county seat of Hickman County, Kentucky] this evening, a right snug little place, built on the hillside of one of the very few bluff banks that run to the river's edge.

Pass Columbus, [Hickman County, Kentucky] which seems to have had some little importance in a business point of view, as here terminates or rather commences the southern extension of the great Illinois Central Railroad. The Mobile Railroad arrives at Cairo about ten o'clock P.M. but soon proceeds up the Ohio.

Thus we have passed over 100 miles, down the great Mississippi River and back, and on all the clearings, fields, and farms, on her rich bottoms, did not see the first vestige of anything growing for food for man or beast (if we except grass and weeds) and on but one or two places did we see any signs of anything like the cultivation of the earth. The towns along its banks look old, desolate and shabby, and nearly

---

[49] "Island Number Ten, The Siege Of", *Encyclopedia Americana*, 1963, XV, 414k.

BY THE DIM AND FLARING LAMPS:
THE CIVIL WAR DIARY OF SAMUEL MCILVAINE

everything that is artificial wears a look of desolation. Much of this however is doubtless attributable to the recent heavy floods.

This evening Amos W. Nash of our company takes suddenly worse and fears are entertained for his life. As to myself, I continue to feel pretty comfortable, but weak; my appetite, however is becoming almost ungovernable.

Friday, May 30, 1862

Quite pleasant this morning. Gets rather warm toward evening.

We run last night during the night and land at Paducha [Paducah, seat of McCracken County, Kentucky] this morn at daylight.

On getting up this morning, I learn that Amos Nash died during the night. We make but a short stop at Paducha [Paducah]; it will be remembered that our forces early took possession of this place and held it until after the evacuation of Columbus by the rebels, and commanded both the Ohio and mouth of the Tennessee Rivers. It seems to be a place of considerable business, and a town of considerable size, but what I can see of it from the river, has an old and weatherbeaten appearance.

As we pass up, saw mills and machine shops line the river banks for some distance. Here is the mouth of the Tennessee River, broad and beautiful. A very narrow tongue of land divides it from the Ohio for some distance up. Twelve miles farther up and we pass the mouth of the Cumberland, which now that the waters are down looks hardly wider than a creek.

Smithland [Livingston County, Kentucky] I have already described on a former trip. The island here, now that the waters are down, appears to have a good farm and buildings on it.

Passing on up, Golconda [Pope County] on the Illinois side glitters below.

Several little towns are pass[ed] on either side, conspicuous among them was Shawneetown [Gallatin County] on the Illinois side, a little below the mouth of the Wabash.

THE DIARY
MAY ENTRIES

We pass the mouth of the Wabash at sundown. Here is a most beautiful island, called Diamond Island from its shape, and here at last we come in view of our native State again. The mouth of the Wabash looks very narrow, hardly wider I thought, than it is hundred of miles up. Possibly it appears narrow to me because of being on the Ohio and the broad Mississippi.

Passing on up we pass, Mt. Vernon in Indiana, the first town above the mouth of the Wabash & county seat of Posey County.

About ten P.M. I go to bed, feel pretty well.

Saturday, May 31, 1862

Becomes quite warm today.

We run during the night and arrive at Evansville, Indiana, at daylight. Here those who had been provided with furloughs before leaving their regiments let off to go on their way to their homes & friends rejoicing. But the rest of us (who now began to see our recently inspired hopes of soon meeting dear friends wane) were ordered to the recently established hospital at Newburgh, [Warrick County,] Indiana, some ten or twelve miles above here.

I do not go ashore here [at Evansville] and can see but little of the city, as the riverbank hides it from our view. The stores, warehouses, etc. seem to have moved back considerably from the water's edge since I first saw them on our trip to Nashville. The city seems to be a place of considerable business and of considerable size, and it is the county seat of Vanderburgh County, Indiana. The river here makes a very short curve or bend to the north. The city is built on the rising bank circling around with the bend of the river, and hence it is frequently called the "Crescent City".

We arrive at Newburgh about nine o'clock A.M. and are landed after a stay of a week on the boat, during which time we had come down the Tennessee from near the Mississippi & Alabama line, passed down the lower Mississippi for over 100 miles and back, then up the Ohio to this point. I could not but contrast the beautiful banks of the Ohio,

BY THE DIM AND FLARING LAMPS:
THE CIVIL WAR DIARY OF SAMUEL MCILVAINE

dotted here and there with cozy little towns, pleasant rural scenery, shady hillsides, and grassy banks, and [the] dirty, shabby looking towns of the lower Mississippi.

A large hotel, and one or two other large buildings nearby are here fitted up as hospitals. I was assigned a berth with a clean comfortable cot to sleep on in the third story of the hotel. Everything looks clean, fresh, and comfortable; dinner came, and it has been a good while since I sat down to such a dinner. Among other things on the table was lettuce, the first green thing I have tasted this spring (if I except spoiled meat). Everything about the hospital seemed clean and made as comfortable as possible; but what lends a charm to it above everything else is the fact that the cooking and waiting on tables is done by women and girls. It appears truly a home for the sick soldiers and alas there are many who have come here among us who need the kindliest attention of the most skillful nurses to preserve their lives.

I make a little excursion through the town this evening, find it a much prettier little place than I had anticipated.

When it became known that a boat load of sick soldiers had landed and entered the hospital, we were visited by crowds of the fair sex, who almost showered us with the bouquets of roses and flowers, and we were made to feel by everything we saw and met with that we had *indeed* landed among friends.

Had a fine shower of rain this evening. Wrote a letter this evening to Capt. Van Natta informing him of the death of Nash and where we were, etc.

June Entries

Here the pages of the original diary began to be worn and some pieces of the pages are entirely lost; where a _____ appears, it indicates that words were missing on the original pages of the diary.

Sunday, June 1, 1862

Very pleasant today.

Take a smart walk this morning, find the town and surburbs really beautiful; pass many yards and gardens fancifully decorated with a great variety of roses, beautiful flowers and shrubbery. Visit a smart field of growing corn, which I saw in the distance. It is the first I have seen and looks beautiful; on my way back pass groups of well dressed and lovely looking children going to Sabbath School. Such scenes I have not been wont to see lately, and they forcibly remind me of the beauties and pleasures of domestic society, such as I have been a stranger to, and especially of my own dear little [children?] at home. What wonder I should drop tears of melancholy joy.

I also once more have the privilege of going to the place where worship and adoration is offered to the great Author of our being, whose name I have for a long time hardly heard mentioned except in a vain and reckless manner. And although the minister (Presbyterian) preaches strong fatality [predestination], yet it was a house of worship, and I felt that it was good to be there.

Another boat arrives with sick soldiers, the Indianians are put off here, and fill our hospital buildings entirely full. I intended to write to my friends today, but having no paper, ink etc. and no chance to buy today, I take another walk this evening and at dark attend prayer meeting at the Methodist Church. In all the prayers I heard today and tonight, petitions were put up for the sick soldiers, and indeed these people seem determined to make us feel at home.

BY THE DIM AND FLARING LAMPS:
THE CIVIL WAR DIARY OF SAMUEL MCILVAINE

Monday, June 2, 1862

Cooler this morning. Pleasant through the day. Walk around a little today, but I spend most of the day in writing home. Write a long letter to my cousin [Mary?] McIlvaine. [One] or two of the poor fellows sent here die today. I continue to feel tolerably well, but ___ s___ ___g appetite, that I can hardly control it.

Tuesday, June 3, 1862

Pleasant today, with a light sprinkle of rain.
Finish writing a letter to my wife and children, mail my letters, (this evening being first since Saturday) walk around etc. this evening.
Don't feel so well ... a painful diarrhea set on me today.

Wednesday June 4, 1862

Cool, damp, and rainy today.
Take a smart little walk this morning. But before going far, begin to feel so bad I wish myself back [at the hospital] again. Begins to rain & I stop in at the mill (which I happen to be near) until the shower is over.
I afterward call at Professor Freeman's at his invitation, learn that he has been professor in several different colleges in the South of late years, and last in Missouri whence he was obliged to fly for safety on account of his love for the Union. Here I find the first number of a publication by Torrey, of the rise and progress of the rebellion, which he offered [to] me to read, and which I find very interesting.
Get back to hospital, eat a bite of dinner, and lay on [my] cot the balance of the evening, my diarrhea [being much] worse.
___ two more soldiers die today, ___ fellows they came too late to the hospital for ___dness of _____.

THE DIARY
JUNE ENTRIES

Thursday, June 5, 1862

Cool and damp today.
Feel quite unwell this morning. Do not go down for breakfast, remain in bed most of the day. The doctor calls ... [and] prescribes some powders for my diarrhea which fail to reach me until ... the evening.

Friday, June 6, 1862

Still cool and damp today.
Feel better [this] morning. Slept pretty well last night. My diarrhea appears to be checked. But I remain in [my] room and my bed most of the day. Read [some].

Saturday, June 7, 1862

A very pleasant day, cool, and a fine breeze.
Get up pretty early, wash and feel better. Write and mail, (before mail goes out) a letter to my sister Abigail. Also one for my comrade J. Riley. Two other poor fellows die today.
Walk out again a little this evening, calling [at] Mr. Phelp's well to get a good drink of water. [Get] into quite an interesting conversation with a young lady here in regard to the varieties, and qualities of the roses in their beautifully ornamented yard, and on starting, she plucked and gave me a fine bunch of them. Read some, etc.

Sunday, June 8, 1862

Very pleasant today. Walk out some through town to view the flowers and shrubbery and pleasant rural scenery which surrounds this place. Commence writing a letter to my Aunt Collins _____ Oskaloose, Iowa, but quit it to go to church (Methodist). Rest upon my

BY THE DIM AND FLARING LAMPS:
THE CIVIL WAR DIARY OF SAMUEL MCILVAINE

cot a part of the day. Read some etc. One week has now passed since we arrived here, and the prospect for making a short visit home has entirely vanished, it appears. Some of the soldiers have [abused] their privilege while on sick furlough and therefore an order is issued against furloughing atta____.

Monday, June 9, 1862

A beautiful day. Take a walk this morning up the river bank, passing a coal pit, the shaft for which is sunk far below the river ____ thence in to a fine wheat field and corn field; as I came back, stop in at workshop and make a fine pair [of] crutches for one of our boys. Read, rest, etc.

Tuesday, June 10, 1862

Warm today. Finish writing and mail my letter to my aunt. Make another pair crutches, read, walk out, etc.
Here I rest for the present, because my book [deteriorates?].

Presumably, the bound volume in which he was writing had reached a section where water damage made it impractical to continue writing, and we can only presume that he continued his diary in another volume.

Letter of September 29, 1862

The following letter, written to Samuel's mother about four months later than the last entry in the diary, was found in the effects of his son William at William's death in 1940.

The envelope was addressed to Mrs. Mary McIlvaine, Oxford, Benton County, Indiana. The verses on the envelope were a song "On Guard" and seem to be a patriotic specialty in envelopes, carrying different songs.

Louisville, Kentucky
September 29th, 1862

Dear Mother & Friends:
With the greatest pleasure I this morning take my pen to address you a few lines again. I feel very sure a few lines will be gladly received from me after so long a time.

Immediately on our arrival here, or the next morning, I sent by James Godman of our company, who started to Lafayette, Indiana, a letter I had written at Nashville, but which I could not send then as the mails were cut off by the rebels getting between Nashville & Louisville, and destroying the railroad bridges. I merely had time to note in pencil, in that letter, our arrival here. I hoped you would get that letter by Tuesday's (tomorrow's) mail. Day before yesterday

BY THE DIM AND FLARING LAMPS:
THE CIVIL WAR DIARY OF SAMUEL MCILVAINE

evening, I received three letter[s], one from Aunt Dianah, dated August 29th; one from Uncle Mosses & Mary McIlvaine dated also August 29th, and one from Jane dated August 31st. These are the only letters I have received since some time before I left the hospital at Evansville, Indiana, although when we got to Nashville I heard from home through Sam'l Martindale, but on receiving Jane's letter I find it is dated a few days after she saw him in Lafayette, but on his way here. So that, her letter *now* a month old, is the last news I have from home. But we can have uninterrupted mails again now, and I hope soon to get late word from home.

The letters from Aunt Dianah, Uncle and Mary, represent, the friends as well as [the] usual uncle's letter, says Wallace was at Baton Rouge at the late battle there, but his company was some three miles out on picket, and missed getting in the battle, but he said he should write to you soon, and he has probably given you the particulars.

In a former letter to Aunt Dianah, I expressed a strong hope that she would if possible make you a visit this fall. In the one I received from her, she intimated a possibility of doing so, but at the same time expressed a fear of going there on the account of her health. I hope you will have the happiness of again meeting her. She says she recollects *well*, in the time of her afflictions, how grateful the company of a dear sister would have been to her. I think if health permits you will see her.

Since the arrival of Gen. Buell's army here, there have been many happy meetings of old friends & acquaintances, between the old and the new regiments; I think there was hardly a man in our regiment who did not meet with a brother, friend, or old acquaintance in some of the recently formed regiments which we found here on our arrival.

I spent several hours yesterday with George & Thomas Freeman & Peter Johnston, who came to see us and took dinner with us. If I had time and room I might describe the dinner & the circumstances under which it was eaten; but I forbear particulars at present, for more important matters. Jack McDaniel of the 60th [Indiana] Regiment (most of which regiment were captured last week by the rebels at Green River) was here yesterday, he happened to be left here; also Clayton

LETTER OF SEPTEMBER 29, 1862

Wilkinson, of same company (whom I have not yet seen) when the regiment were sent to Green River. All the balance of their company were captured. This regiment is badly cut up (I mean disorganized or scattered). We passed two or three companies of it at Bowling Green.

I presume you have heard through the papers of the capture of some 4,200 of our troops at Green River last week, by the rebel forces under Bragg, Buckner, Hardee & others. Well, most of the 60th Indiana Regiment (as I have said) were captured there, including most of the boys from about Oxford and Benton County who were in it. We were making a forced march from Bowling Green to reinforce them when they surrendered. We were too late, but met them after they were paroled and on their way to Bowling Green where the rebels sent them. Col. Jack Templeton, Capt. J. Burns, Marion McConnell, Volney Wilkinson, Walter Sargent [Sarjent?], were among those I had the pleasure of taking by the hand. I had time but for a few words with them, as our regiment was marching one way and they the other; though glad to see them I was sorry to meet them as prisoners of war. There [were] many other of my acquaintances with them but in the crowd and hurry I did not get to see or speak to them. They were to go to Bowling Green; thence make their way to the Ohio River just above Evansville. Such was the course marked out for them by the rebels. They thence go to you, Cincinnati, or to Camp Chase, probably to be exchanged. They were all well as far as I learned.

In the early years of the war, it was not uncommon for prisoners to be "paroled", with the requirement either that they not participate further in the war, or to take a circuitous route home before again participating in the war.

This process of exchange was formally discontinued by the Union in late December, 1862, for a variety of reasons, including the treatment of black soldiers captured by the Confederacy. Special exchanges were continued until May, 1863. Man-for-man exchanges were resumed in January,

BY THE DIM AND FLARING LAMPS:
THE CIVIL WAR DIARY OF SAMUEL MCILVAINE

1865, since the Union captured many more prisoners than the Confederacy.[1]

William Marion McConnell (1828-1916): William was the twin brother of Samuel's wife Margaret Jane McConnell; William moved to Indiana with his parents at the same time as Margaret. March 1, 1849, William married Margaret Sarjent. In 1852, William and three other men travelled to the California gold fields via covered wagon. William spent more than a year in California, returning by way of Panama and New York City.

William enlisted in the 60th Indiana Volunteers, Company D, in 1861, later serving in the 147th Indiana Volunteers, Company K. Like Samuel's wife Margaret, William's wife Margaret moved into Oxford for the duration of the war. Unlike Samuel, William returned from the war.

William and Margaret moved back to their farm outside Oxford and lived there until Margaret's death (1912) and William's death (1916). William and Margaret had ten children.[2]

Samuel refers to a Walter Sargent; while there is no documentation to support it, it seems to me likely that the last name was actually Sarjent, and that he was a brother of Margaret Sarjent McConnell.

There were several friends and acquaintances here whom I have not yet seen. Milton Sarjent, the Dinwiddie boys, Ira Brown, Amos Jarvis, Jordon Roberts, Jas. Freeman, Will Stanley, and I know not

---
1 Long, p. 716.
2 Bartindale, pp. 25-26.

LETTER OF SEPTEMBER 29, 1862

how many others. Clay Cassell was in our camp evening before last, the boys are all well so far as I have seen or heard. I have not been out of camp (except to get water) since we arrived, I felt very weary and rather unwell the day after we got here Saturday last & it rained most of the day. I therefore did not feel much like running around.

On Sunday (yesterday) we were required to stay in camp to sign the payrolls. Today we are expecting to be paid, receive clothing, etc. I therefore as yet have had no chance to see any of the boys only those who came to our camp. I now have about $100 coming to me, but it must be recollected that I borrowed some $35 the last I sent home, this I must replace, and if we get our pay, I will try to send most of the balance home.

I intimated in the few lines I wrote after we got here, that I had not been well for a few days; the day we got to Bowling Green, we got very wet, and as it continued to rain till after dark, and we having no tents (having turned them over to another regiment at Nashville), we had to lay on the wet ground & in our wet clothes. I took a little cold; a night or two after while on picket I had a light chill and for a day or two some fever. I took a good dose or two of medicine, and have not since been bothered with fever; but I was a little fearful for a few days that I was going to have a recurrence of ... diarrhea, but a few days rest & chance to change [diet], or rather get a suitable diet, has removed that.

I was a little surprised short time since whilst busily writing at this letter, to see Marion McConnell, Volney Wilkinson, Keys & one or two others, of the 60th Regiment who were taken prisoners the other day at Green River and whom I have said already we met south of there going to Bowling Green, walk into our camp here. They tell us they went to Bowling Green thence through Litchfield, and Big Spring, & struck the Ohio River at Brandenburgh 40 or 50 miles below here & thence came up here. They complain of having a hard march, in this ground, with but little to eat. They got here last night. They think they will possibly get to go home a short time or at least be sent to Indianapolis to be exchanged or reorganized. I find I have filled this sheet and hardly spoken of that [matter] I [wished to speak of] to you.

BY THE DIM AND FLARING LAMPS:
THE CIVIL WAR DIARY OF SAMUEL MCILVAINE

I must therefore write you a few more lines on another page. If we stay here a day or two longer, I will write again to Jane and others.
Evening.
There was an unfortunate circumstance [that] took place this morning resulting in the death of [Brig.] Gen. Nelson; there are but few in the army (so far as I have heard, an expression) that seem to mourn him heartily. All who have been under him seem to have regarded him as a tyrant; & according to the report we got of it, he was stigmatizing the Indiana soldiers, saying he had on a certain occasion cut off one of their heads; when Col. Jeff Davis of Indiana said he was an Indianian & did not brook insults to Indianians. At this, Gen. Nelson gave him a slap in the mouth when [at which] Col. Davis drew his pistol and shot him dead immediately.

The incident was rather more colorful than Samuel describes. Major Gen. William Nelson (1824-1862)[3] "... was a huge ox of a man -- three hundred muscular pounds on a frame six feet four, a man who alternately glowed with hail- fellow geniality and stormed with titanic rage." Brig. Gen. Jefferson Columbus Davis (1828-1879) (not to be confused with the similarly named Confederate President), had been rebuked by Nelson, and after an argument in a Louisville hotel lobby (in which Nelson had slapped Davis), Davis returned with a revolver and shot Nelson.

Gen. Buell (Nelson's superior) requested that Davis be tried for murder. Davis was never tried by the military, primarily because of the influence of Indiana Gov. Morton, who had been with Davis during the argument and already held Gen. Nelson responsible for the defeat at Richmond in late September. The case was referred to the civil authori-

---
[3] Boatner, p. 586.

LETTER OF SEPTEMBER 29, 1862

ties, but a grand jury refused to indict him. In the end, Davis was never punished, and eventually promoted.[4]

Our paymaster did not make his appearance today in our camp, but is expected tomorrow. It is now rather thought we will remain here several days, as Buell's army are receiving a new outfit of wagons, cooking utensils, clothing, blankets, etc. preparatory to starting out again.

Since I commenced writing this, the mail came in bringing me a letter from Abigail dated September 9th; this speaks of her being quite sick, but I yesterday read a letter from her to George of a later date wherein she speaks of having been quite sick, but was then better. I hope soon to hear of her entire recovery.

But what pains me most is to hear of *your* continued ill health; Jane wrote to me that all the friends were well as usual "except Father and Mother" but whether she meant Mother McConnell or *you*, she left me to guess. She speaks of you being at Hainsville a few days with Abigail, which leads me to think you are not down sick; but the tone of all the letters I have received for sometime from home tells of a trouble; *a great and terrible one on your mind.* I am sorry *truly* to still hear the sad news; and tired & weary indeed, must I be at night when I lay me down to rest upon my lowly couch upon the ground, if I forget to invoke God, if consistent with His good will, to remove that great affliction & trouble from the mind of dear and venerated Mother, and permit me to meet her again upon Earth; and I most truly have an abiding faith that He will do it.

Oh! that I had words to infuse this faith into your mind. It is true I feel an anxiety to live yet a little longer in this world, with all its vanities, follies, and sinfulness, and wretchedness; I feel a desire to live that I may do some good, that I may do my part to alleviate the suffering and sorrows of poor fallen humanity; but I fear *not* to die, and leave this world, feeling conscious that when I go hence, be it sooner or

---

4 Catton, p. 8-10.

BY THE DIM AND FLARING LAMPS:
THE CIVIL WAR DIARY OF SAMUEL MCILVAINE

later, I shall still find employment of perhaps a far more noble character.

Yet it is ill with this world and [with] the thing[s] of this world we have not to deal. It is for our own happiness & welfare, the happiness and welfare of our fellow mortals, of our children, and our children's children that we are now to labor. God grant that I may not shrink from the responsibilities resting upon me; did I not fully believe the work I am engaged in a justifiable one, and one of imperative duty, to all the lovers of liberty and light in the world, one that must not be shrunk from; then would I abandon it. But 'tis useless to argue this matter. Suffice it to say, that to abandon the cause I am now engaged in, and acknowledge the right of a portion of the people of the United States to sever, or rive in twain, and destroy this Government, which stands out to the rest of the world as the polestar, the beacon light of liberty & freedom to the human race; would be to undo all that I have ever learned, all that I have ever been taught in regard to the rights and privileges of the human race. Therefore I believe our cause to be the cause of liberty and light, to the masses of mankind, the cause of God, and holy and justifiable in his sight, and for this reason, I fear not to die in it if need be.

The envelope on this letter was sent to me by Aunt Dianah with a request to send it to my family. I therefore send [it] to *you*. The verses have a touch of sorrow it is true [but] are beautifully and singularly appropriate, and you may oft have them read by some of the children.

Your unworthy son, Sam'l

May God's Blessings and protecting care continue to rest upon all of you.

Across the top of one sheet was written: "The Union shall be preserved!"

BIBLIOGRAPHY

Anonymous, "Zollicoffer, Felix Kirk", *Encyclopedia Americana*, 1963, XXIX.

_____. "Brownlow, William Gannaway", *Encyclopedia Americana*, 1963, IV, 621-622.

_____. "Buckner, Simon Bolivar, Jr.", *Encyclopedia Brittanica*, 1983, Micropaedia II, pp. 340-341.

_____. "Fort Pulaski", *Encyclopedia Americana*, 1963, XI, 514b-514c.

_____. "Halleck, Henry Wager", *Encyclopedia Americana*, 1963, XIII, 646-647.

_____. "Harlan, John Marshall", *Encyclopedia Americana*, 1963, XIII, pp. 709-710.

_____. "Island Number Ten, The Siege Of", *Encyclopedia Americana*, 1963, XV, 414k.

_____. "Rosecrans, William Starke", *Encyclopedia Brittanica*, 1983, Micropaedia VIII, 672-673.

_____. "Rosecrans, William Starke", *Encyclopedia Americana*, 1963, XXIII, 696.

Bartindale, Ethel McConnell, *McConnell Family History*, (Oxford, Indiana: privately printed, 1923), pp. 24-25.

Biel, John G., ed., "Notes and Documents: The Battle of Shiloh: From the Letters and Diary of Joseph Demmet Thompson.", Tennessee Historical Quarterly, vol. 27-3, pp. 250-274.

Billings, John D., *Hardtack and Coffee or The Unwritten Story of Army Life*, (Williamstown, MA: Corner House Publishers, 1973), p. 348.

Boatner III, Mark M. , *The Civil War Dictionary* (New York: David McKay Company, Inc., 1959).

Brooks, Stewart, *Civil War Medicine*, (Springfield, IL: Charles C. Thomas Publishers, 1966).

Catton, Bruce, *Glory Road*, (Garden City: Doubleday & Co., 1952).

Floyd, John B., "Report of Brig. Gen. John B. Floyd, C. S. Army," in *The War Of The Rebellion: A Compilation Of The Official Records of The Union And Confederate Armies*, Series 1, ed. Lt. Col. Robert N. Scott, (Washington: Government Printing Office, 1882), VII, p. 428-429.

BIBLIOGRAPHY

Foote, Andrew H., "Report of Flag-Officer Andrew H. Foote, U. S. Navy", in *The War Of The Rebellion: A Compilation Of The Official Records of The Union And Confederate Armies*, Series 1, ed. Lt. Col. Robert N. Scott, (Washington: Government Printing Office, 1882), VII, p. 423.

Grant, Maj. Gen. U.S. , Letter to Capt. N.H. McLean, in *The War Of The Rebellion: A Compilation Of The Official Records of The Union and Confederate Armies*, Series 1, ed. Lt. Col. Robert N. Scott, (Washington: Government Printing Office, 1882), X, part 1, p. 109.

Jordan, Winthrop D., Litwack, Leon F., et. al., *The United States Conquering A Continent*, 5th ed. (Englewood Cliffs, NJ: Prentice-Hall, 1982).

Long, E. B., *The Civil War Day By Day*, (Garden City, NY: Doubleday & Co., 1971).

Mitchell, John B., "Island Number 10", *Encyclopedia Americana*, 1984, XV, 510.

Nevins, Allan, *War For The Union*, (Charles Scribner's Sons, 1959).

Ripley, Warren, *Artillery and Ammunition of the Civil War*, (New York: Van Nostrand Reinhold Co., 1970).

Sword, Wiley, *Shiloh: Bloody April*, (New York: William Morrow & Company, 1974), p. 60-61.

Thornbrough, Emma Lou, *Indiana in the Civil War Era 1850-1880*, (Indianapolis: Indiana Historical Bureau & Indiana Historical Society, 1965).

Weems, John Edward, *To Conquer A Peace*, (Garden City, NY: Doubleday & Co., 1974).

INDEX

Alexander County, Illinois, 127
Apples, 96, 99, 127
Army of the Cumberland, 61
Army of the Ohio, 77

Bardstown, Nelson County,
   Kentucky, 9, 34, 36, 37
Baton Rouge, Louisiana, 141
Battle of Buena Vista, 40
Battle of Fishing Creek, 9, 14
Battle of Laurelhill, Virginia,
   61
Battle of Logan's Cross Roads,
   9
Battle of Mill Spring, 14, 67,
   118
Battle of Shiloh, 89, 98, 101,
   105
Bear River, 101
Bell, John, 3, 52, 53
Benton County, Indiana, 2, 44,
   142
Black suffrage, 76
Bluemass, 92
"Bogus senators", 129
Boonsport, Kentucky, 46
Bowling Green, Kentucky, 53,
   55, 68, 108, 142, 144
Brandenburg, Meade County,
   Kentucky, 46, 144
Brownlow, William Gannaway,
   76
Buckner, Simon Bolivar, 32, 41
Buell, Don Carlos, 14, 44, 45,
   51, 72, 75, 141, 145, 146

Cairo, Alexander County,
   Illinois, 127, 132
Calliope, 46, 52
Calomel, 90, 92, 123
Campbellsville, Taylor County,
   Kentucky, 21, 27
Canister, 70, 118, 119
Cannellton, Spencer County,
   Indiana, 46, 47
Canton, Trigg County,
   Kentucky, 51
Capsicum fructescens, 123, 124
Caseyville, Kentucky, 48
Cathartic, 90, 92
Cave, 21, 22, 23
Chase, Salmon P., 82
Chattanooga National
   Cemetery, 5
Chickasaw, Alabama, 101
Cider, 31, 33
Clarksburgh *see* Clarksville
Clarksville, Montgomery
   County, Tennessee, 53
Clifton, Wayne County,
   Tennessee, 97
Cloverport, Kentucky, 47
Collective nouns, 7
Colt's revolver, 15
Columbia, Adair County,
   Kentucky, 10
Columbia, Maury County,
   Tennessee, 84, 87, 106
Columbus, Hickman County,
   Kentucky, 65, 66, 108, 128,
   132, 133

INDEX

Concordia, Kentucky, 46
Conestoga, 130, 131
"Congestion of the bowels", 66
Constitutional Union Party, 53
Corduroy roads, 28, 108, 125
Corinth, Alcorn County,
    Mississippi, 103, 107, 110,
    111, 112, 113, 117, 119,
    123, 124
Corn planting, 98
Corn, Cracking, 78, 83
Cots Creek, 37
Cotton, 46, 63, 77, 78, 83, 96, 101, 102
Cotton Gin, 78
Craft, Betty, 41
Crawford County, Indiana, 46
Crittenden County, Kentucky, 50
Crittenden, George B., 13, 14
Crittenden, John J., 14
Crittenden, Thomas L., 14
Cumberland Ironworks, 52
Cumberland River, 9, 11, 32, 45, 49, 50, 51, 52, 54, 55, 97, 133

Danville, Boyle County, Kentucky, 29, 30, 32
Davis, Jefferson Columbus, 145, 146
Derby, Perry County, Indiana, 46
Diamond Island, 134

Diarrhea, 93, 97, 110, 112, 137, 138, 144
Dick's River, 30
Dougherty, Rev. George T., 36
Dover, Stewart County, Tennessee, 52, 53
Duck River, 86, 87
Dycusburg, Crittenden County, Kentucky, 50
Dyersburg *see* Dycusburg

Economy, 51
Eddyville, Lyon County, Kentucky, 51
Electing company officers, 73, 80
Elizabethtown, Hardin County, Illinois, 48
Emancipation Proclamation, 33
Epsom salts, 88
Evansville, Vanderburgh County, Indiana, 126, 134, 141, 142

Fishing Creek, 26
Fitch, Graham N., 8, 128, 129
Foote, Andrew H., 32, 54
Fort Donelson, 32, 35, 41, 52, 53, 54
Fort Henry, 32, 126
Fort Pillow, 127, 128
Fort Pulaski, 104
Franklin, Williamson County, Tennessee, 77

INDEX

Fredericksburgh [Fredericktown], Washington County, Kentucky, 37
Frog music, 91
Fry, Speed S., 13, 31, 101

Ginning apparatus, 78
Glendale, 43, 44
Golconda, Pope County, Illinois, 48, 133
Gov. Wickliffe's Meadow, 38
Grant, Ulysses S., 32, 41, 61, 89, 101
Great Southern Railway, 53
Green River, 141, 142, 144
Guard mounting, 86

Hall's Gap, 29
Halleck, Henry Wager, 108
Hard bread, 33, 34, 92
Hardin County, Tennessee, 46, 48, 95, 99
Hardin's Creek, 97
Hardtack *see* Hard bread
Harlan, John Marshall, 20
Hawesville, Hancock County, Kentucky, 47
Hawsville *see* Hawesville
Hickman County, Kentucky, 128, 132
Hickman, Hickman County, Kentucky, 132
Hoiden School, 87

Hurricane deck, 44, 46, 47, 48, 52

Indian Creek, 90
Indians, 45, 50
Island No. 10, 86, 128, 131, 132
Island No. 18, 131

Jackson, Mississippi, 123
Jeffersonville, Clark County, Indiana, 45

Kansas-Nebraska Act of 1854, 96
Kentucky River, 30
Kentucky State Guard, 41
Kise, William C., 29, 39, 67, 91, 117, 118, 122

Lady Pike, 43, 44, 50, 54
Lafayette, Tippecanoe County, Indiana, 43, 44, 140, 141
Lebanon, Marion County, Kentucky, 10, 16, 28, 31, 33, 36, 65, 106
Lewisport, Hancock County, Kentucky, 47
Lice, 79
Livingston County, Kentucky, 49, 133
Long roll, 12, 18
Louisiana Purchase, 60, 95

INDEX

Louisville, Kentucky, 30, 37, 39, 40, 41, 42, 43, 45, 48, 53, 58, 140, 145
Louisville and Nashville Railroad, 9
Louisville, First settlement of, 45
Lyon County, Kentucky, 51

Manson, Mahlon Dickerson, 5, 30, 37, 39, 67, 71, 72, 74, 80, 81, 91, 122
Maury County, Tennessee, 79, 84, 87
Maxville, Maxville, Indiana, 47
McCook's Division, 77, 78
McCook, Alexander, 77
McCracken County, Kentucky, 133
Meade County, Kentucky, 46
Memphis and Charleston Railroad, 101
Memphis, Tennessee, 66, 67, 129
Mercurous chloride *see* Calomel
Mexican War, 13, 29, 40, 60, 108
Mill Springs, Wayne County, Kentucky, 18, 34, 35, 36, 37, 40, 41, 42, 43, 45, 51, 67, 69, 72, 80, 111, 118
Miller, A.O., 39, 67, 112
Mississippi River, 127, 128, 129, 132, 134, 135

Missouri Compromise of 1820, 60, 95
Mobile Railroad, 132
Mortar boats, 130
Morton, Oliver Perry, 120, 122, 145
Mound City, Pulaski County, Illinois, 127
Mount Washington, Bullitt County, Kentucky, 40
Mt. Pleasant, Maury County, Tennessee, 87
Mt. Vernon, Posey County, Indiana, 134
Muldrow's Hills, 29
Mule meat, 117
Murfreesboro, Rutherford County, Tennessee, 71

Nashville, Tennessee, 44, 45, 51, 55, 59, 62, 71, 80, 87, 140, 141, 144
National (Gold) Democratic Party, 42
"Necessity is the mother of invention", 110
Negroes, 62, 79, 94
Nelson County, Kentucky, 10
Nelson, William, 145
New Albany, Floyd County, Indiana, 45
New Amsterdam, Harrison County, Indiana, 46
New Haven, Nelson County, Kentucky, 10

154

INDEX

New Madrid County, Missouri, 128
New Madrid, New Madrid County, Missouri, 128, 131
New Orleans, 102, 104, 110
Newburgh, Warrick County, Indiana, 134
Northwest Ordinance, 60

Ohio & Mississippi Railroad, 53, 127
Ohio City, 128
Ohio River, 3, 43, 45, 48, 49, 50, 127, 132, 133, 134, 142, 144
Oilcloth, 19, 34, 47, 109, 116
"One of Lincoln's hirelings", 57, 60
Oskaloose, Iowa, 119, 138
Ottoman Army, 11
Oxford, Benton County, Indiana, 2, 44, 73, 140, 142, 143

Paducah, McCracken County, Kentucky, 133
Palmyra, 53
Paroled, 142
Payrolls, 68, 69, 72, 78, 80, 82, 83, 113, 144
Penitentiary, 7, 45, 74
Perry County, Indiana, 46
Perryville, Boyle County, Kentucky, 33
Photographic studio, 107

Pine Village, Warren County, Indiana, 111
Pittsburg Landing, 98, 99, 101, 125
Polk's tomb, 59
Polk, James Knox, 57, 59, 60
Pope County, Illinois, 48, 133
Posey County, Indiana, 134
Prisoner exchange, 41
Prisoners, 13, 67, 117, 122, 142, 143, 144
Prussian Army, 11
Pulaski County, Illinois, 127
Pulaski County, Kentucky, 9, 10, 21

Quinine, 104, 123

Rebel prison, 76
Regiments:
    Hosskin's Regiment *see* Kentucky 12th
    Indiana 9th, 68
    Indiana 10th, 2, 29, 30, 37, 43, 61, 106
    Indiana 14th, 106
    Indiana 15th, 68, 75, 86
    Indiana 34th, 128
    Indiana 40th, 86
    Indiana 43rd, 128
    Indiana 46th, 128
    Indiana 47th, 128
    Indiana 60th, 144, 145, 146, 147
    Indiana 147th, 143

INDEX

Iowa 15th, 119
Kentucky 1st, 19
Kentucky First Calvary, 19
Kentucky 4th, 12, 13, 43, 65, 91, 100
Kentucky 10th, 19, 20, 23, 65
Kentucky 12th, 19, 27
Michigan 11th, 37
Minnesota 2nd, 12, 43
Ohio 1st Calvary, 93
Ohio 9th, 12, 43, 81, 82, 86
Ohio 14th, 39, 40, 65
Regulars 18th, 81, 82, 83, 86, 93, 121
Wolford's Calvary *see* Kentucky First Calvary
Regulars, 82
Rockport, Spencer County, Kentucky, 47
Rolling Fork Salt River, 9, 29, 37, 38, 46
Rome, Perry County, Indiana, 46
Rosecrans, William Starke, 61
Runaway slaves, 32, 33
Rutherford County, Tennessee, 71

Sabbath School, 136
Salt River *see* Rolling Fork Salt River
Saltpeter Caves, 5, 23
Sam'l Gaty, 98
Sassafrass, 110

Savannah, Hardin County, Tennessee, 99
Schoepf, Albin Francisco, 11, 14, 27, 122
Shawneetown, Gallatin County, Illinois, 133
Sherman, William Tecumseh, 110, 112
Sibley tent, 61, 62
Siege of Island No. 10, 132
Skirmish at Widow Serratt's, 122
Slave hunters, 3, 32
Slavery, 3, 4, 53, 59, 60, 76, 95, 97
Slaves, 4, 32, 33, 62, 64, 78, 83
Smith's Fork, Hardin County, Tennessee, 95
Smithland, Livingston County, Kentucky, 49, 50, 133
Sommerset, Pulaski County, Kentucky, 9, 10, 11, 19, 21, 25, 27, 28, 45, 80, 81
Southern Railway, 40, 53
Southern Rights parties, 58
Spelling, 6
Spoiled meat, 5, 135
Springfield, Washington County, Kentucky, 36
Springhill, Maury County, Tennessee, 79
Stalactites, 3, 22
Stalagmites, 3
Stanford, Lincoln County, Kentucky, 29

INDEX

Stephenson, Chaplain, 68
Stephensport, Breckinridge County, Kentucky, 46
Stewart County, Tennessee, 51, 52
Sutler, 103

Telegraph, 10, 109
Tell City, Spencer County, Indiana, 47
Tennessee River, 32, 52, 55, 97, 101, 126, 133, 134
Tennessee State Militia, 35
Tennessee Statehouse, 56, 57, 59
Texan Rangers, 68
Thompsonville, Breckinridge County, Kentucky, 46
Tiptonville, Lake County, Tennessee, 128, 131
Tobacco, 96
Tobaccoport, Stewart County, Tennessee, 51
Treaty of Paris, 60
Trigg County, Kentucky, 51
Troy, Spencer County, Indiana, 47
Tying up a man by the thumbs, 81, 82

Underground explorations, 22, 23
Underground gallery, 21
Underlined words, 7
Union loyalty oath, 41

Van Natta, Job H., 29, 67, 68, 69, 72, 73, 80, 82, 107, 111, 135
Volunteer regiments, 82

W. W. Crawford hospital boat, 125
Wabash River, 48, 97, 133, 134
Washington County, Kentucky, 36
Washington's birthday, 36
Wayne County, Tennessee, 89, 97
Waynesboro, Wayne County, Tennessee, 89
West Point, Hardin County, Kentucky, 46
Williamson County, Tennessee, 77

Yorktown, Virginia, 102, 106, 110

Zollicoffer encampment, 9, 11
Zollicoffer, Felix Kirk, 11, 13, 14, 27, 31, 55, 79

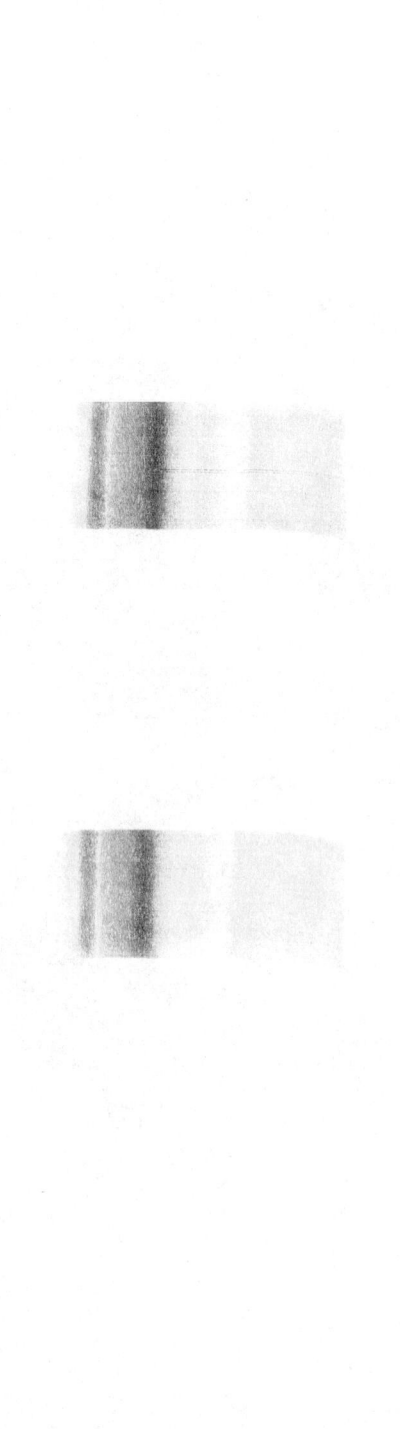